EVERGREEN CEMETERY

CEMETERY

of Santa Cruz

EVERGREEN CEMETERY
of Santa Cruz

TRACI BLISS

with Randall Brown

THE
History
PRESS

Published by The History Press
Charleston, SC
www.historypress.com

Front cover, clockwise from top left: Belle Dormer; Scott family plot, for whom Scotts Valley was named. *Photo by Heather Grimes*; Memorial for Fleck and Denison families. *Photo by Gary Neier*; Men of the Congregational Chinese Mission; Frank and Lillian Heath.
Back cover, top to bottom: Detail of Sawin Memorial. *Photo by Gary Neier*; Seth Blanchard; Restored arch at Dia de Muertos celebration, 2019. *Photo by Kate Clark*.

First published 2020

Manufactured in the United States

ISBN 9781467143868

Library of Congress Control Number: 2020930481

Notice: The information in this book is true and complete to the best of our knowledge. It is offered without guarantee on the part of the authors or The History Press. The authors and The History Press disclaim all liability in connection with the use of this book.

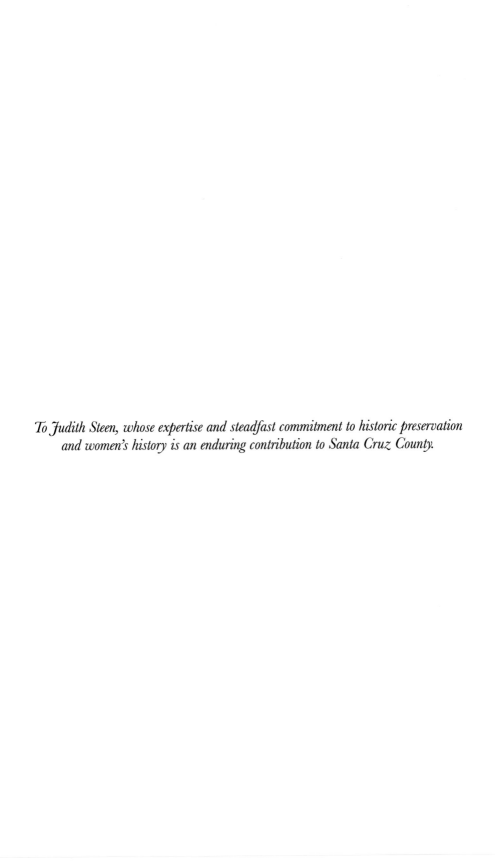

To Judith Steen, whose expertise and steadfast commitment to historic preservation and women's history is an enduring contribution to Santa Cruz County.

CONTENTS

CONTENTS

CONTENTS

ACKNOWLEDGEMENTS

I've been fortunate to have two indispensable resources for exploring Evergreen's past: preservationist Judith Steen as a mentor and the *Evergreen Cemetery Preservation Plan* as a "big picture" guide. Also essential has been the productivity of several individuals whose work, spanning decades, provided a rich foundation for the stories I tell: Dana Bagshaw, Geoffrey Dunn, Ross Gibson, Rick Hyman, Sue Kerr, Margaret Koch, Sandy Lydon, Joan Martin, Joe Michalak, Robert Nelson, Ernest Otto, George Ow Jr., Norman Poitevin, Marion Pokriots, Phil Reader, Martin Rizzo, Leon Rowland, Stan Stevens, Carolyn Swift and Paul Tutwiler.

Descendants of men and women who were buried at Evergreen early on—Nancy Kilfoyl Campeau, Jim Lorenzana, the Newcomb and Schupbach families and Casey Tefertiller—shared detailed family stories and photo archives. Their generosity and great help enabled me to create multigenerational sagas, as inspiring as they are diverse.

The chapters titled "Evergreen's Renaissance" and "Families Then and Now" offer a window into several years of consistent and extensive restoration efforts by Evergreen Committee volunteers. I am indebted to Nancy Campeau, Kate Clark, Bob Dahlgren, Sangye Hawke, Anne Hayden, Frank Hayden, Judy Jones, Cynthia Mathews, Mary Jo May, Gary Neier, Dave Newcomb, Sibley Simon, Winston Spedding and Mary Wood. In addition, Ms. Mathews and Ms. Jones lent me their meticulous document collections. The Santa Cruz Museum of Art and History's (MAH) curator of history, Marla Novo, serving as the Evergreen Committee chair, made available many unique photographs from MAH's exceptional archive. I want to give much-deserved thanks to the MAH Publications Committee for the many Santa Cruz County History Journals, from which I drew essential context for the 1800s. For rare documents and key source materials, generally unavailable elsewhere, the reference collection and newspaper indexing project of the Santa Cruz County Genealogy Society have been invaluable.

I am honored to have received a grant from the Santa Cruz County History Forum; contributions from individual Forum members Nancy Campeau, Burt Rees and Mary Wood; and the 2018 Dolkas/Mertz Award—all of which helped to support dedicated consultants. My heartfelt thanks to editor Martha Mee Dunn, genealogist Marion Pokriots, historian Randall Brown and photo production manager Gary Neier and his wife, Tara. Special appreciation goes to Laurie Krill, Arcadia/History Press acquisitions editor, for her confidence in an untested idea and Elizabeth Humphrey, my niece, for her wisdom and encouragement. My watchful feline companions, Bella and Paws, supplied much-needed levity at critical junctures.

Prologue

GATEWAY TO THE PAST

J ames Imus—the first person buried at what would ultimately become Evergreen Cemetery—died at age nineteen in 1853. My maternal grandmother, Belle, told me a bit of the story. "To protect the memories of James and his uncle, Captain Charles Imus, interred in 1856, our Imus ancestors donated their land for a cemetery open to all." As an inquisitive ten-year-old, I wanted to know more, but my mother dismissed any questions, adamant that our connection was too distant to matter and the graveyard too insignificant to visit. We took her admonition to heart: it would be fifty years before I ever set foot in Evergreen, and my brother on the East Coast never has.

After my mother's passing, my indifference to Evergreen took a radical turn when I discovered the name on Belle's birth certificate didn't match the name she'd always used. I felt compelled to investigate those "too distant to matter" relatives. Unearthing the well-hidden family secret sent me on what genealogist Marion Pokriots—my sixth-grade teacher—called a sacred journey.

My grandmother, an only child, never once mentioned her father. A bigamist, he was apparently expunged from the family record soon after his sudden desertion of six-month-old Belle and her mother to marry another woman. Learning this from poring over Santa Cruz county records and documents at the Family Research Library in Salt Lake City, I began piecing together my unknown relationship to Evergreen. Belle always remarked on the goodness of Judge Henry Rice and his wife, Lucy Imus Rice, my great-great-great-grandparents, who helped build Santa Cruz in the early 1850s. But the anecdotes never meant much to me until, bolstered with new information, I explored the Rice family plot at Evergreen with its beckoning obelisk. What had Belle meant by the "the Rices' goodness"? Tracking down third cousins I'd never met, they explained that the judge and Lucy sheltered their granddaughter—Belle's mother—from the intense shame she endured as an abandoned woman with an infant during the Victorian era.

Once I started down the path of exploring the burial ground's past—to better understand my own—I couldn't stop. Delving into the uniqueness of the men and women who coalesced to create a city and its surrounding towns became irresistible. From the moment of its founding, Evergreen evolved as an epic story of commitment: of parents to children preceding them; of Masons to their brethren; of soldiers to their comrades; of Chinese to their ancestors; and of the thousands of volunteers who have helped maintain the cemetery for over a century to honor those who went before.

Some individuals portrayed in these pages have been the stars of Evergreen history tours for decades. Here we tell their stories from a fresh perspective while sharing the enduring contributions of many others, not as biographies but rather as interlaced lives that helped mold the values of a very young and evolving town. If well-known pioneers do not appear, it is not because they were less important. Rather, we selected from a wide group of individuals, some better known and some lesser known, reflecting the diverse aspirations, occupations, vocations, ethnicities and cultures that intertwined to create Santa Cruz. Nearly two thousand additional residents are buried at Evergreen; I hope this modest beginning inspires the telling of their stories as well.

Note: In the following chapters, all the individuals buried at Evergreen will have their names underlined the first time they appear in the text.

Chapter 1

THE POTRERO

Geologically speaking, Evergreen Cemetery won't rest in peace. It rides the Pacific plate, close to where it collides with North America, as does the entire town of Santa Cruz. Ancient earthquakes shaped the location, uplifting a slab of seafloor to form a ninety-foot-tall, flat-topped ridge. The graveyard occupies the side of the hill, overlooking a broad floodplain, stretching out eastward to the San Lorenzo River.

Storms coming in from the ocean drop significant amounts of rain on the coastal hills and mountains. The boundaries within and around Evergreen are partly defined by water courses, one running along the edge of the steep "Glory Path" and another separating the family plots of its main section from the "Potters' Field."

When the Santa Cruz Mission was established in 1791, the padres occupied all the lands on the west side of the San Lorenzo River, including the present site of the city of Santa Cruz. "We have enclosed the place for cattle, sheep and horses," they advised their superiors, "and we have fenced the orchard."[1] Subsequently, the flat land below Evergreen's hillside became known as "the Potrero" (pasture).

The Potrero provided a fertile home for farm animals—as many as 131 oxen, mules and saddle horses. Predators prospered. "There were many bears in those days," Lorenzo Asisara, born and raised at the mission, remembered. "They used to come and sit on their haunches on the hill (overlooking the Potrero and today's cemetery), watching for a chance to kill one of the calves of the mission."[2]

In 1833, the Mexican government passed the Secularization Act, terminating the mission system; Governor José Figueroa spelled out how to "fairly" distribute the mission properties. The "new citizens" (neophytes)— the name applied to natives brought into the mission over its three decades of existence—were granted homesteads. The northern section of the Potrero was deeded to a group of vaqueros and their families. Some of its land, however, was reserved for the village to have as common pasture. After the "new citizens" received their share of the mission properties, the rest of its territory became part of the public domain. Local officials and other well-connected residents quickly claimed for themselves the most desirable locations. The natives as well as the priests tried to slow the process, asking that the orchard and the adjacent pasture be maintained for the benefit of the community.

By 1847, when Americans took charge of Santa Cruz, most of the land in the vicinity had already been parceled out. Alcalde (mayor) <u>William Blackburn</u> decided that the church had a right to possess only the land bounded by the walls of the former mission. His definition included the orchard but not the common corral in the Potrero. That land, once legally granted, set the stage for Evergreen Cemetery's creation.

Chapter 2

EARLY ARRIVALS

Buried at Evergreen are several members of the earliest, pre–gold rush wagon trains whose journeys west demanded undaunted determination, stamina and resourcefulness. For example, the saga of Mary Patterson's wagon train, the first to successfully make it over the Sierras, reveals remarkably tenacious women. And the Imus Party's experience in 1846 raises the consequential question: whom do you trust when faced with a potential life-or-death decision? Many risk-taking pioneers prospered in Santa Cruz, but they also endured some heartbreaking losses as they crafted the identity of their town and the surrounding communities.

NEVER A DULL MOMENT

Isaac Graham, shaped by his adventures as a fur-trapping mountain man in the 1820s and '30s, adapted to new circumstances with ingenuity and dramatic flair. No wonder! The rough life of those early pathfinders to the western frontier brought them into unending perils where death could be around the next corner. Graham arrived in California in 1833, most likely as a member of the Joseph Walker Party. As the first expedition to make it across the Sierras, the men endured a host of challenges and had to eat their horses to survive.

Isaac Graham commissioned this portrait of himself at the height of his fame in the early 1850s. *Courtesy of California State Library, Sacramento.*

Before actually settling in California, Graham went back to his prior home in Tennessee. He returned with the two items essential for his business plan. The first—a portable copper still—he used to open a distillery at Natividad, conveniently located on the well-traveled road between Monterey and San Juan Bautista. This distillery became a popular destination for young Californios like Juan Bautista Alvarado. Graham's second innovation—the introduction of a Tennessee racehorse to the Central Coast—generated more than a few contests with local vaqueros and ranch owners.

In the fall of 1836, Alvarado led a local revolution against the Mexican government and asked Isaac Graham to organize his trapper friends to support the effort. While Alvarado's group surrounded the town of Monterey, Graham's men surprised the nearby fort. Though the coup was remarkably bloodless, when negotiations began to fail the following day, a cannon shot crashed through the roof of the governor's headquarters. A prompt surrender ensued, and the campaign ended when the government in Mexico City decided to accept Alvarado as the new governor.

Although they were initially allied against the enemy, relations between the empowered Californios and the well-armed riflemen soon deteriorated. "I was insulted at every turn," Alvarado recalled, "by the drunken followers of Graham."[3] In fact, Graham insisted that the governor resented him not for his alcohol production but for having won twenty-two horse races in a row![4]

As it happened, rumors convinced Alvarado that Isaac Graham had plans to organize Americans and Englishmen to murder all the Californios (second generation of Mexican or Spanish descent) who were at least seven years old. Subsequently, Alvarado ordered a raid on foreigners at Graham's Natividad distillery. A wounded Graham was imprisoned in Monterey in 1840. Soon after, Mexican authorities shipped him and forty-five other "troublemakers" off to a Mexican prison, presumably for good. But thanks to the efforts of a British consul, their release came within a year.

The next move for the trapper-turned-entrepreneur would be trying his luck at Zayante in the Santa Cruz Mountains. There, a former friend from his mountain man days, Joseph Majors, ran a sawmill. Having lost considerable property at Natividad, Graham jumped into the lumber business and acquired half the ownership of the Zayante Rancho, near today's Roaring Camp. At age forty-five, being somewhat settled in the lumber business, he was ready for romance. Whence would it come?

A Young Pioneer Woman's Saga

A St. Louis newspaper ran an article titled "American Paradise,"[5] advertising the beauty and grand opportunity California offered. Months later in 1843, the Chiles-Walker Party departed from Missouri. Recruited to join the migrant company were the Williams brothers—four hardy young men. Once in Idaho and short on supplies, the brothers, along with Chiles and eight other men, split off from the larger group to journey by horseback. Their grueling trip, filled with hardships and the hazards of living off the land, prompted a twentieth-century historian's awe: "This little horseback party might be said to have served as a school for guides and explorers."[6]

After arriving at Sutter's Fort in 1844, the older brother, James Williams, gladly accepted an offer of free land near the future site of Stockton. But his livestock venture turned disastrous when his friend and partner Thomas Lindsay was killed under horrific circumstances.

Meanwhile, his eventual bride, <u>Mary Patterson</u>, would have an even more harrowing—and, to many, "miraculous"—experience getting to the "American Paradise." Families at the then-extreme edge of the United States dreamed of the mild climate farther west. For some, migrating became a necessity after a malaria epidemic swept through the swampy border regions of Missouri. In 1844, trapper Isaac Hitchcock, part of the Walker Party almost a decade earlier, accompanied his widowed daughter Elizabeth Patterson and her five children as part of the Murphy-Stephens-Townsend Party. Mary, age fourteen and the eldest daughter, tended to her younger siblings during what one party member called "a rash undertaking, for at that time no trail over the mountain was known."[7] The company of fifty, from ten families, wisely elected veteran trapper Elisha Stephens captain.

When the migrants encountered Caleb Greenwood, the crusty, foul-mouthed, eighty-year-old mountain man who guided fur traders over the Sierras, he escorted them to Nevada's Humboldt Sink. But it remained to be seen how they would find a route over the daunting mountains beyond. Greenwood did his part, connecting the group with Chief Truckee of the Paiutes. The tribal leader firmly believed that all men are brothers, descended from a common ancestor. His communications with Captain Stephens consisted mostly of diagrams on the ground to show a path over the mountain range.

The travelers first camped at what would later be called Donner Lake and then began the arduous climb toward the Sierra summit. But with snow falling and confronted by what seemed an impassable vertical granite ledge, the party considered abandoning their wagons. Captain Stephens prayed earnestly "and was granted a vision on how the pass could be surmounted." They discovered an opening "just wide enough to allow one ox to pass." As soon as the oxen made it through, the animals were then positioned to pull from above. As "the men heaved up on the wheels from below…the emptied wagons were taken up, one by one."[8]

Following the immense joy of getting safely over the summit, the pioneers faced a life-threatening reality. The heavy snowfall made traveling as a party impossible. The women and children, assisted by a few men, would have to stay behind with the wagons. With her brood of five, Elizabeth Patterson was now stranded for the winter at the Yuba River, but she figured out how to keep her children alive. "Suffering considerably from hunger,"[9] eventually their only option was boiling hides for food, and for two weeks, they ate nothing but the glue-like substance. Finally, the rescue party arrived in March and escorted the resilient group to Sutter's Fort. Though severely

In the 1890s, the Murphy family hired San Jose artist Andrew P. Hill to portray the wagon train led by Captain Elisha Stephens. *Courtesy of Sourisseau Academy for State and Local History, San Jose State University, San Jose, California. A.P. Hill Collection.*

Sutter's Fort provided shelter and supplies to overland migrants. This lithograph is based on an 1846 sketch by navy lieutenant J.W. Revere. *Courtesy of National Park Service.*

malnourished, every woman and child had survived the fierce winter. It had been nine months since they'd departed from Council Bluffs on the banks of the Missouri River. Historian Kevin Starr calls the Stephens Party's journey "that great dazzling success! But all of that was forgotten under the power, the dystopian power of the Donner Party," two years later.[10]

With available women in very short supply, Mary Patterson could probably have had her pick of the men she met at Sutter's Fort. Did James Williams succeed in capturing the attention of the teenager, half his age, through their connection as native Missourians? After a whirlwind courtship, she became Mary Patterson Williams on August 24, 1845, the first American couple to be married in California. American consul Thomas Larkin presided over the well-attended ceremony in Monterey. With roses abounding in the area, perhaps fifteen-year-old Mary embraced the tradition of tossing the bride's bouquet. And perhaps her guest Catherine Bennett caught the flowers!

Is Romance Contagious?

While visiting Isaac Graham's Zayante Rancho soon after the Williams wedding, the twenty-one-year-old Miss Bennett became enamored with the forty-five-year-old firebrand. A friend of Graham's proclaimed, "The hardy veteran is…about to cast away the deathly rifle and the unerring tomahawk for the soft smiles of a female companion to nourish him in his old age."[11] All the same, their impromptu civil ceremony on September 26 caused quite a stir. Consul Larkin claimed the unofficial rites were illegal and urged Alcalde José Bolcoff "to remove her from the house of Mr. Graham."[12] Bolcoff replied, "Graham said…he would not separate from the side of Bennett, that he would lose a thousand lives before he would give her up. You well know the character of Graham. He never likes to obey any authority."[13]

Captain John Frémont may have been the only authority figure Graham ever respected. On a rainy February day in 1846, the captain and Kit Carson rode to the Zayante Rancho. Now on his third expedition— ostensibly a scientific mission—Frémont was keen to determine the actual species of the *palo colorado* (redwood). Hosting the two men amid days of downpour, Graham showed off the most impressive tree in the grove of giants. "He named it the Frémont Tree and cut the letter 'F' deeply in the bark."[14] This gesture symbolized Graham's most significant contribution to Santa Cruz County history. Rain or shine, he welcomed the American presence and helped provide safety for the earliest pioneers. The Mexican authorities, quite aware of Graham's precision with a rifle, never set foot in the Santa Cruz Mountains, where Graham unofficially presided. Five years after Frémont's visit, a dream Graham worked hard to realize came true. In 1851, he received more than $30,000 from the Mexican government to compensate for his lost property. The settlement earned the former trapper quite a reputation and enabled him to buy the remainder of the Zayante Rancho, land he held until the end of his life in 1863.

Meanwhile, James and Mary Williams would have the tragic distinction of being the first family unit buried at Evergreen. Having moved to Santa Cruz County after their wedding, the devastating story began when James, in partnership with his brother Squire, bought "twenty Spanish acres on the extreme southern boundary of the Sanchez tract" (part of the old mission farm) and the four-and-a-half-square-mile Rancho de la Laguna from James Dunleavy.[15] There, the brothers became the earliest lime producers on the North Coast, eight miles from Santa Cruz. By the age of nineteen, Mary had two young sons to bring up on the remote rancho. At age twenty-one, she went into labor, hoping to give birth to twins, but any medical help was hours away by horseback. Despite the best efforts of family members, Mary did not survive. Within a year, James suffered two more blows: first, a large drop in the price of lumber and then the deaths of his twin boys. In 1852, he buried them next to his beloved Mary on the Laguna property.

James married Pauline Rickmer, a woman of considerable means, three years later. With a fresh start for James, the newlyweds moved to Williams Lane (today's Lincoln Street) in downtown Santa Cruz. Cultivating his extensive acreage on Pacific Avenue, he produced peaches, apples and enormous twenty-pound onions. When Pauline visited her family in Germany for an extended stay, evidently James did not communicate despite her attempts to make contact. Then, at age forty-five, he died of lung disease, and his 1858 funeral at Evergreen was one of the first at the newly created cemetery. One source claimed that James suspected his wife might have wished him dead, perhaps by poisoning, so he ordered an autopsy in the event of his death.[16] The coroner could provide no such evidence. Most significantly, James Williams's final wishes were to be reunited with his original family. Mary and the two twin boys, Andrew James and James Andrew Williams, were removed from their Rancho Laguna graves and reinterred in the Williams plot.

THE MAN FOR ALL SEASONS

Of all the early settlers in Santa Cruz, no one would wear as many different hats as the six-foot-four Virginian <u>William Blackburn</u>. With friends, including <u>Henry Speel</u>, he left St. Louis in the spring of 1845 to join the Swasey-Todd Party of mounted men, carrying only the most basic gear on packhorses. Originally bound for Oregon, Swasey convinced his group to alter their course and head to the sparsely populated California instead. Blackburn, up for the adventure, later told a reporter, "We felt confident it would soon become American territory and wished to be in time to get the benefit of the transfer."[17] And he would benefit enormously, so much so that at one time five locations in Santa Cruz County bore the name Blackburn: a creek, a gulch, an irrigating dam, a lagoon and a terrace.

The Swasey-Todd Party did not experience the usual trials of other pioneers. When Blackburn, a skilled cabinetmaker, and Speel arrived in Santa Cruz in the early fall of 1845, they immediately began working in the lumber business for Isaac Graham at Zayante. Graham welcomed the newcomers, who enjoyed his plentiful homemade whiskey while listening intently to his assessment of precarious local politics: the Mexican authorities planned to expel Americans, of whom there was a sizable group living in the Santa Cruz Mountains. Captain John Frémont's visit to the area with Kit Carson exacerbated the tensions. Soon after, the American settlers at Sonoma raised the Bear Flag, and Lieutenant Blackburn and Sergeant Speel joined the revolt against the Mexican government. The two friends rode with Frémont's California Battalion to Buenaventura (today's Ventura), where the lieutenant is said to have fired the first cannon shot against the Mexicans.

William Blackburn, a visionary and versatile entrepreneur, made his mark in a variety of businesses, the law and politics. *Courtesy of MAH.*

Under the terms of secularization, the Santa Cruz Mission's properties had been distributed a decade earlier. Property reserved for the church included only buildings inside the mission compound. Despite the vehement protests of the presiding priest, the adjacent structures quickly became rowdy saloons. Back from the war, Blackburn and Speel enjoyed the Mission Plaza entertainment hub and wanted more of it. With his keen eye for opportunity, the former lieutenant opened the Eagle Hotel in a two-story building on the plaza, using one of the rooms for a general store that stocked imported Chinese goods.

A man on the move, Blackburn became the first alcalde to serve under American rule and was rebuked by the acting governor for his unorthodox court pronouncements. During the gold rush, he voluntarily vacated that post to manage his burgeoning businesses in San Francisco and Sacramento. Blackburn built a vast network of contacts well beyond Santa Cruz due to his leadership within the statewide Society of California Pioneers, which required a member to have arrived in California prior to 1850.

Of Blackburn's many ventures, including a tannery, sawmill and fruit orchard, he probably received the most recognition for the fortune he made growing potatoes on land that is downtown Santa Cruz today. But William Blackburn's commercial good fortune could not be replicated in his family life (see page 56).

MASS MIGRATION, NATIVE PEOPLE AND COWBOY ENTREPRENEURS

The *Emigrants' Guide to Oregon and California* by Lansford Hastings described a California with near-perfect climate where American residents would soon "throw off the Mexican yoke."[18] In the spring of 1846, hundreds of wagons began the migration west, responding to Hastings's call. Among the pioneers were Adna Hecox and his wife, Margaret, accompanied by three wagons carrying their adventurous neighbors: Joseph Aram, his wife and three children; and forty-five-year-old bachelor Charles C. Imus with his teenage nephew Charlie. Along the route, others joined in. According to Aram, "It became necessary to elect a man to take the command of the company; we elected Charles Imus as captain, he having had some experience with the Indians in the Black Hawk War."[19] In fact, Imus, who respected his former enemies, had befriended them at the conflict's end.

Aram wrote of the captain's prowess with a local tribe not far from Fort Laramie. "Nearly two hundred [were] coming towards us at full speed and yelling loudly, Captain Imus advanced…with rifle in hand, motioned for them to halt. They obeyed instantly; he motioned for the chief to advance. He came a few steps forward; the captain laid down his gun, and then motioned for the chief to do the same. They advanced until they met, then shook hands. There was but little doubt at the time that the prompt action of our captain saved us trouble."[20] Nonetheless, Imus knew his limitations, and the party soon hired Caleb Greenwood, the guide for many previous migrants.

At Green River, Wyoming, the party connected with a much larger group from Illinois led by George Donner. One of the Donner Party members, James Reed, already a fan of Lansford Hastings, agreed with the young adventurer's advice that all of them should take a shortcut south of the Great Salt Lake. Aram had no idea the significance of the event he then recorded: "Hastings advised us by all means to go that way, assuring us that we would save a month's travel, but our old pilot, Greenwood…told us that it would be much safer to go by Fort Hall. After much talk, many of the emigrants took Hastings' advice, particularly the Donner Party."[21] Instead, Captain Imus trusted the seasoned guide, having no interest whatsoever in a route where wagons had never been. The self-assured Reed, when writing to a hometown paper, attributed the decision of Imus and others to "being afraid of Hastings' Cut Off."[22]

After piloting the Imus Party to Fort Hall, Greenwood gave them an introduction to Chief Truckee, who offered to guide them across the Sierra Nevada range. In contrast to earlier wagon trains, this time, the chief and some relatives wanted to join in and see California for themselves. As the migrants climbed foreboding mountain passes at Truckee's direction, he and Captain Imus formed a friendship. Then came urgent news from Sutter's Fort: the outbreak of the Mexican War. As soon as the wagon train reached the Sacramento Valley in late September, the party's unmarried men, including the Imuses, enlisted in the California Battalion, serving under Frémont's command until their discharge at the conclusion of the 1847 campaign.

Now free to pursue their dreams, Charles and Charlie Imus concocted a grand plan. At the junction of the San Joaquin and Stanislaus Rivers, they erected a large corral for their "wild horse" scheme. But after James Marshall's discovery of gold in January 1848, chasing wild horses to tame and sell seemed rather far-fetched when compared with the lure of gold. Yet all they discovered was the backbreaking work of mining. Just a few months later, the cowboys returned to the life they had known.

Selling high-priced horses and beef to prospectors, the duo could afford a bit of leisure and spent the last months of 1848 in Santa Cruz, reconnecting with members of their wagon train and scouting the real estate market. The Imus men and a friend paid $2,100 in gold for a piece of the old mission

This engraving of "Old Chief Truckee," who befriended and guided many pioneer parties, appeared in Thompson and West's 1881 *History of Nevada*.

farm, a bottomland tract. The broad area stretched along the west side of Pacific Avenue (then Willow Street) from today's clock tower down to Church Street and all the way up to Chestnut Street.

With spring in the air, hundreds of forty-niners descended on the Imus ranch on the San Joaquin, paying top dollar for livestock. Charles and Charlie, relishing very deep pockets, decided to move to Santa Cruz permanently. They'd barely settled in when they invited more than twenty family members of every age to join them in the promised land.

The cowboys' second priority was how best to capitalize on the local chaos created by the rush for riches. Land grants issued by Alcalde Blackburn were conditional: claimants had to fence in their lots and build houses within a year. Although much of the Potrero had been parceled out, a large tract adjacent to the mission orchard remained unclaimed. Blackburn awarded it to his friend Alfred Baldwin, but he failed to meet the required conditions. Charles and Charlie immediately petitioned the alcalde's office to be granted the Potrero land, which was ideal for livestock and an all-purpose farm.[23] Substituting for Blackburn, the interim alcalde happened to be Adna Hecox, the Imuses' close friend from their overland journey. When Hecox approved their request, Baldwin said "not so fast" and filed a counterclaim. A court hearing resulting in a cash settlement eventually gave title to the Imus men. That single transaction set the foundation for Evergreen, first as a family burial ground and then as an "open to all" cemetery.

Chapter 3

PROTESTANT PIONEERS

BUILDING COMMUNITY FOUNDATIONS

Doggedly pragmatic, Methodists were the first settlers to establish a church, school and business district in Santa Cruz, embracing every opportunity to share their faith. "Above all Methodism grew because it wanted to and because those who carried out the missions considered themselves as sacred emissaries in the spread of scriptural holiness across the land. In this task Methodists encountered little structural opposition. In the American West there were no established churches, a seemingly endless supply of new people and new land, and a relative undersupply of cultural institutions."[24]

The flexible church structure included the election of lay preachers to serve as ministers in newly developing towns. In early 1848, Elihu Anthony, recently arrived from Indiana, served in that role for the twelve-member congregation. Shortly after settling in, he and another adherent, Benjamin Case, successfully claimed vacant real estate on today's Front Street, an area most regarded as worthless, swampy bottomland. The ambitious Christians, eager to rein in the robust appetite for liquor, established the first Temperance Society in California, designating Case as chairman.

Whatever plan Anthony and Case had for downtown was put on hold. As news of the discovery of gold at Sutter's Fort spread like wildfire, prospecting for souls became a lesser priority. With her husband off at

Civic-minded activists Benjamin and Mary Amney Case were among the earliest settlers in Santa Cruz and part of the group who founded the Methodist church. *Courtesy of MAH.*

the mines with Anthony, <u>Mary Amney Case</u> exemplified the aspiring Methodist woman. In the disproportionately female denomination, women were allowed and even occasionally encouraged to have a public voice. Zealous about education and an experienced teacher, Mary single-handedly opened the first school in Santa Cruz. She welcomed children of all faiths to the multi-age classroom, located in her home adjacent to Neary Lagoon. Among the fifteen pupils were her two sons and the sisters of Mary Patterson Williams. The first official public school opened five years later, with Benjamin Case, back from the mines, serving as trustee along with Hiram Imus Jr.

Death Valley Survivors

With the rush to California in full swing, John and Abigail Arcan and their infant son Charles left Illinois for the gold fields in April 1849. They, and three other families, decided to take a shortcut after leaving Utah. But that fork in the road led to the treacherous sands of Death Valley, a 120-mile-long basin, as yet unnamed. The Sand Walking Company, as they called themselves, found little potable water, and the situation grew even worse with dwindling supplies. Moreover, Abigail could not comfort little Charles. "Having a whole body red as fire with illness"[25] he had to be carried on his father's back. Two young men who'd joined the expedition, William Manly and John Rogers, volunteered to leave the valley on foot to find food and water for the others. After a difficult three-week journey, the pair returned with beef, beans and flour, enough to stave off starvation. Desperate to escape the desert, the party abandoned their wagons and their cherished possessions. Abigail, holding Charles, rode one of the few oxen not killed for food. As they reached the edge of the basin, one of the party, looking back, said, "Goodbye, Death Valley,"[26] and the name stuck. "Manly and Rogers' feat is one of the most heroic rescues in California History."[27]

When the Arcans finally arrived in Santa Cruz, Abigail was captivated by the scenery and homelike environment. "You can go to the mines if you want to," she told her husband. "I have seen all the God-forsaken country I am going to see, for I am going to stay right here as long as I live."[28] The family, devout Methodists, received a warm welcome from Mrs. Case and others in the local congregation. As it happened, the church's newly appointed minister and his wife, James and Julia Brier, had been their companions in the Death Valley ordeal. Mrs. Brier's cheerful solicitude had helped them all survive, and in gratitude, when Abigail gave birth to a daughter on July 1, she named her Julia. Tragically, the baby died only nineteen days later.

Above: Zabriskie Point in Death Valley illustrates the type of treacherous terrain encountered by the Arcan family in 1849–50. *Photo by Ron Clausen.*

Right: Julia Arcan, who lived for nineteen days, was originally buried in the Methodist graveyard on Green Street in the 1850s. This recently restored headstone reflects her reinterment at Evergreen in the 1860s. *Photo by Kelly Manning.*

"Professor of Aquatic Natation" Charles Arcan proudly displays his swimming awards and lifesaving medals. Photo preserved by Mrs. Fred Harder. *Courtesy of Bear State Library.*

Julia Arcan's beautifully restored headstone bears the earliest date, 1850, of all the memorials at Evergreen, but most evidence suggests that the first burial on that land came later. The Methodists had established a burial ground in back of their recently constructed church, and it is highly likely that, as members of the congregation, the Arcans interred her there, where they could visit regularly after Sunday services. When a new, larger church replaced the original building in 1863, it became necessary to move the bodies buried on the site to Evergreen, where John and Abigail had purchased a family plot.

Forsaking the temptation to chase gold and eager to provide stability for Abigail, John Arcan constructed a building at the corner of today's Pacific and Soquel Avenues, consisting of his carpentry and gunsmith shop, rooms for his family and an upstairs meeting room for the local Masonic Lodge. Julia's brother Charles, having recovered from the hardships of Death Valley, grew into a strong and healthy young man. His wholehearted participation in the early culture of Santa Cruz included a stint as swimming instructor at the Neptune Baths. Charles enjoyed his title—"Professor of Aquatic Natation"—as did the prominent Californians among his clientele, such as Leland Stanford. The railroad tycoon gave Charles a gold-headed cane as a reward for rescuing him from a near-drowning.[29] Although he moved to San Francisco in the 1890s, Charles frequently returned to Santa Cruz to visit his widowed sister, Abbie Arcan Flores, and to care for the family plot where John, Abigail and Julia were buried. He was laid to rest next to them in 1907.

AN ORDEAL RESULTS IN ROMANCE

The Arcans weren't the only future Santa Cruzans to be stranded in the unforgiving California desert. Because Charles and Charlie Imus painted "such bright pictures of the land of gold,"[30] many of their clan headed west together in early May 1849. Three generations set out from Galena, Illinois: Charles's parents, Hiram Sr. (approaching eighty) and Ruth (then sixty-one); their daughter Malvina Imus Rice, her husband, Philip, and their six children; and Charles's brother Hiram Imus Jr., his wife, Eliza, and eleven of their twelve children.

Due to unforeseen delays, the party decided not to risk a wintertime crossing of the Sierras, instead heading south toward Los Angeles. But nothing would go as planned; Malvina gave birth early to her seventh child in the bleak terrain southwest of Salt Lake City. The boy received an appropriate pioneer name: Boone Frémont Rice.

Once through the Utah mountains, the travelers encountered the deadly Mojave Desert, where their livestock suffered from a severe lack of water and fodder. Already forced to eat their failing oxen, how long could the family endure? Fellow migrants Ike Holcomb and "Kentuck" Phillips offered to seek help and then journeyed day and night until they reached a ranch near Los Angeles. They begged owner John Rowland for supplies, yet the tough ex-trapper refused, "saying he had already been duped by several parties who told similar tales."[31] But the resolute rescue team, undeterred from their mission, struck an astonishing deal. Holcomb would remain at the ranch under guard, and if Phillips failed to return in a reasonable time, the hostage could be hanged or shot.

Phillips loaded an old Spanish ox cart with flour, bacon and other supplies and crossed 150 miles of isolated desert. Reaching the Imus/Rice camp in the middle of the night, he found the adults awake, bleary-eyed and on the verge of starvation. "Mrs. Imus mixed some flour, water, and salt together, and some pancakes were quickly baked in the frying pan. The children were wakened from sleep and each one received a tiny cake."[32]

Hiram Jr. then led the group to Rowland's ranch, and what a "small world" coincidence that was! Hiram's brother, Captain Charles Imus, had served with Rowland in the Mexican War; moreover, the men had been imprisoned together for several months. While the Imus clan recuperated, the now gracious Rowland invited his guests to make cheese from his dairy, ensuring they were well supplied for their journey north.

Hiram Imus Sr., patriarch of the extensive clan, crossed the plains at age seventy-nine. Venerated as the oldest Mason in California, he lived well into his nineties. *Courtesy of MAH.*

Revitalized, the migrants traveled as far as Ventura, where they buried the infant Boone Frémont, the one devastating casualty of the trip. Weeks later, imagine the joy when the Imus/Rice extended family—twenty-three in all—reunited with Charles and Charlie in Santa Cruz after a four-year separation! Moreover, the saga of deprivation and loss ended with a storybook romance. Ike Holcomb, the young man willing to risk his life as John Rowland's hostage, reappeared. Soon afterward, Emily Imus, eldest daughter of Hiram Jr. and Eliza, married the heroic Ike.

CIVILITY HAS ITS PLACE

Henry Rice and his wife, Lucy Imus Rice, parented five children on their prosperous farm in western Illinois. But Lucy longed for her family, all of whom had relocated to Santa Cruz by 1852. Decisively, she persuaded her husband to migrate. They packed up four daughters and one son, ages three to sixteen, and joined thirteen other California-bound wagons. Following the Truckee trail, the entourage crossed the Sierras without incident.

When the Rices arrived in Santa Cruz, Elihu Anthony and Benjamin Case had already begun the development of today's downtown. Among the new buildings on Front Street was a hotel, the Santa Cruz House, described by a witty observer as "a large commodious building of jaundiced complexion, with a bar room where cocktails are sold."[33] Sizing up the situation, Henry and Lucy purchased an acre of land from her brother Charles and nephew Charlie for $800. The newly arrived couple built Rice's Hotel on the unoccupied west side of Pacific Avenue.

Challenging the competition, Henry advertised their establishment as a "Temperance House" with "NO Bar and NO Billiards."[34] Lucy welcomed sober travelers, who remembered her as "never too tired or weary not to enjoy a joke, telling stories with a freshness wholly her own."[35] Henry Rice soon turned over the entire management of the hotel to the women of his family, Lucy and daughters <u>Charlotte</u> and Jane, to pursue his unexpected calling.

When Santa Cruz County came into being in 1850, William Blackburn accepted election as its first judge but soon stepped down. His successor,

This 1856 drawing by traveling artist Henry Miller is probably the earliest rendering of the village of Santa Cruz. *Courtesy of Bancroft Library.*

Theron Per Lee, apparently had an unseemly approach to the law. An encounter with a long-winded attorney revealed his priorities. "The judge interrupted him by stating that he had an authority to consult. Quietly looking down from the bench he said to his clerk: 'Peter, hand out that authority.' Peter drew from under his desk a large demijohn and three or four glasses."[36] Alas, consulting authority took on new meaning!

Local activist Eliza Farnham blasted Judge Per Lee as "a drunkard and debauchee" who had fathered two illegitimate children during his two years on the bench. "Many of those who had helped to place him in office demanded a change of some sort. They got it. His successor is, I believe, an honest man."[37] Nonetheless, Mrs. Farnham did wonder how Henry Rice had defeated a better-educated candidate. A neighbor explained: "It was his daughters that elected him. There are a great many single men in the county, and the judge's daughters are fine girls. I am a single man myself and I voted for him, though I never expect to ask one of them to marry me."[38] Rice freely admitted his qualifications for the county judgeship consisted of only a few years studying law in Illinois.

He conducted his court on simple principles. "We must acknowledge that law is founded on horse sense and good judgment, and when a man exercises these he will hit the law pretty much every time." For his courtroom style, the

Charles and Charlie Imus, owners of a portion of the west side of Pacific Avenue, sold an acre to the Rice family for their hotel in the early 1850s. The structure burned in 1865, replaced by the Pacific Ocean House shown here with balcony. *Courtesy of Covello and Covello.*

veteran frontiersman embraced improvisation, telling a reporter years later, "We had no set rules. Every man went his own road. The lawyers didn't talk back to me. I'd sock 'em in jail gosh darn 'em."[39] The judge weighed three hundred pounds.

Meanwhile, Rice's Hotel provided comfort and civility for guests wishing alcohol-free lodging. In the summer of 1856, the family enlarged and refurnished the building, surpassing the Santa Cruz House in size and amenities. Though it was in an ideal location for any visitor to the town, the survival of the hotel as a "Temperance House" proved to be short-lived.

Chapter 4

CREATING AN
INCLUSIVE CEMETERY

A BUSTLING, WELCOMING TOWN

As outsiders began to take notice of the thriving village by the bay, the editor of the *Pacific Sentinel* in Monterey found it to be an excellent community. He was duly impressed by the number of churches, schools, Sons of Temperance members and industrious citizens. In the summer of 1856, the paper relocated to Santa Cruz with local entrepreneur Albion P. Jordan providing an incentive: free transportation for the printing press. "A list of eighty-nine paid in advance subscribers was signed and the little printing plant crossed twenty-nine miles of water on the schooner *Queen of the West*."[40]

Jordan hosted an extraordinary celebration the following year when he helped the town open up to the world outside. He and his partner Isaac Davis realized that the surrounding hills contained a trove of mineral wealth: Santa Cruz lime. With soaring demand for their product in San Francisco and Sacramento, they felt stymied by the limitations of the harbor. The pair, needing a better wharf to load lime barrels onto ships, petitioned the legislature. Their friend William Blackburn, now the region's assemblyman, sponsored the successful bill.

Born and raised in Maine, Jordan wasted no time putting his maritime roots to work, overseeing the East Coast construction of the *Santa Cruz*, a fast and elegant steamship. The stunning vessel left San Francisco at noon on July 22, 1857, with a contingent of reporters. Jordan spared no trouble

Left: "Universally loved by those sustaining business relations with him, he was a noble and warm friend, always pleasant and quick with a word from the heart." The *Sentinel* paid this tribute to Albion Jordan in 1867. *Judith Steen Collection.*

Below: This wharf, constructed by lime merchants A.P. Jordan and Isaac Davis in the 1850s, was later owned by Henry Cowell. *Courtesy of MAH.*

to provide those passengers with the ideal Santa Cruz experience. To cap off the grand festivities, he held a ball at the Eagle Hotel featuring a Native American band. Led by Lorenzo Asisara, an accomplished clarinetist, the musicians displayed their versatility by opening with an oratorio by Handel before transitioning to popular dance tunes.

THE PASSING OF VALIANT PIONEERS

For years, Isaac Graham had encouraged prospectors to try their luck near Zayante, and they finally did in 1856. "Our little town," a local correspondent informed a San Jose paper, "has been thrown into a most extraordinary state of excitement by reason of the discovery...of gold-bearing quartz.... No other subject commands attention."[41] Captain Imus relished his new adventure. The mine owned by Charles and his associates hit pay dirt, averaging around $1,000 per week.

The surrounding property, located near the junction of the San Lorenzo River and Zayante Creek, included dense redwoods, home to a robust population of grizzly bears. One of them attacked Imus, inflicting a deep wound. In an 1885 *Sentinel* interview, Sarah Winnemucca, granddaughter of Chief Truckee, recalled the aftermath. At the time, living with Hiram and Eliza Imus, she noted Mrs. Imus's steadfast care for her brother-in-law. But the seemingly invincible Charles never recovered.

His family laid him to rest on their cattle ranch, the Potrero land, near the grave of his nephew James Imus, interred in 1853. It would be a defining moment in the town's evolution. The pioneer's passing opened up Santa Cruz for others to develop today's Pacific Avenue where the cowboy had staunchly maintained his horse-racing track. And for the Imus family, it raised a profound question: two family members, James and Charles, had now passed on prematurely. What could be done to ensure that their memories would be permanently honored?

Fortuitously, the Imus/Rice clan played a prominent role in the town's political infrastructure. Leaders of the local Democratic Party, the family also relished a long association with the main civic organization, the Masons. The lodge sponsored every Fourth of July celebration and in 1857 featured patriarch eighty-seven-year-old Hiram A. Imus, the oldest Mason in California. The townspeople marched to the Imus Grove by the San Lorenzo River for an afternoon of feasting and toasts.

Above: Landscape artist Edward Vischer sketched this view of Isaac Graham's Ranch while visiting the famous Big Trees of Zayante in 1862. *Courtesy of Online Archive of California.*

Left: Restless cowboy Captain Charles Imus met his match encountering a grizzly bear in the Santa Cruz Mountains. His death in 1856 contributed to the founding of the cemetery. *Photo by Gary Neier.*

The parade marshal, J.F.J. Bennett, soon to become the Masonic grand marshal, may have begun an auspicious courtship that very day. Before the year's end, he would marry Jane Rice—the second daughter of Judge Henry and Lucy Imus Rice—a union that solidified the influence of the local Masons and the Imus clan.

Meanwhile, Methodist minister Albert Higbie initiated a significant civic improvement. In an 1857 letter to the *Sentinel*, he argued that the existing graveyard adjacent to his church was no longer sufficient. "Quite a number of families in and about town would like to secure family lots which cannot be done as things now are." Higbie claimed, "Good grounds and ease of access can now be had."[42] Considering what happened next, the reverend's optimism suggests he had been in contact with the Imus family. The tragic death of a well-known pioneer incited a community response.

IMMEDIATE ACTION

Harry Speel, a loyal friend of Judge Blackburn and well-known to the Imus family, lay dead on the beach. The cause was his fall from a forty-foot cliff on the west-side of town. With no room at the Methodist graveyard on Green Street, Speel's friends turned to Hiram Imus Jr. He probably convened most of the adult members of his large clan to affirm his and his sister Lucy Rice's decision. They would offer a burial spot up the hillside from their brother Charles's grave. After the funeral, a man close to Harry Speel declared, "The esteem in which he was held is evinced from the fact that without exceptions the entire population attended his sepulture."[43]

But who might be next? Proponents of a town cemetery jumped into action. "An association for the purpose of procuring a suitable burying ground has been set on foot in Santa Cruz, with every prospect of success."[44] On June 7, 1858, less than a week after the discovery of Speel's body, County Clerk J.F.J. Bennett filed a deed. The new Imus in-law transferred title to approximately seven acres from Hiram A. Imus Jr., augmented by one and a half acres from neighbor James L. Prewitt, to three trustees acting on behalf of the inhabitants of the town of Santa Cruz. To seal the transaction, the trustees paid Imus and Prewitt one dollar.[45]

Then, just six weeks later, the trustees invited citizens of Santa Cruz to the burial ground to purchase choice lots at the newly named Evergreen Cemetery. The name apparently reflected the sponsorship of the local

This early photograph of Evergreen Street shows the recently established cemetery on the left and an Imus family home in the foreground. *Courtesy of MAH.*

Masonic Lodge consistent with their burial rites, in which symbolic sprigs of evergreen are interred with the body. Led by Bennett, the local Masons soon acquired several plots to accommodate their unclaimed or indigent brethren. For his family plot, Judge Blackburn purchased the area where Speel had been laid to rest, ensuring that his companion of so many decades would not be forgotten.

The growing Evergreen population increased by at least fifteen due to reinterments in 1863. Methodist church elders needed the graveyard land for a larger building to accommodate their burgeoning congregation. A widely circulated notice, titled *Removal of the Dead*, stated that "all who have friends buried there may have sufficient notice and time to remove them. All that remain at that time, or are not otherwise disinterred by friends, will be exhumed by the Society and buried in [Evergreen's] Potter's Field."[46]

Evergreen trustee William Cooper advised that lots for reburials could be secured at his Cooper Brothers Mercantile store on Cooper and Front Streets. He offered to provide a key to the cemetery gate, enabling

William Cooper, community leader and Evergreen trustee, offered his land as the site for the county courthouse in the 1860s. The iconic Cooper House opened at that location in 1972. *Courtesy of MAH.*

wagons bearing the remains of loved ones to pass through at their own convenience. Cooper's ethic of service and dedication to his community went well beyond his stewardship of Evergreen. He served as postmaster for several years and became the first mayor of Santa Cruz during the local government reorganization in 1876. According to journalist Margaret Koch, "William befriended the few Mission Indians who were left....He no doubt slipped many a sack of flour or bag or beans or warm blanket to some hungry, cold Indian."[47]

Chapter 5

AGRICULTURE GROWS UP

THE FERTILE DOWNTOWN

When Santa Cruz officially became a township in 1850, it boasted a population of 643. Of the 211 men who cast votes in the first election, "55 were of Mexican-California descent; 51 were settlers of pre-gold-rush-days and 105 were forty-niners."[48] Shortly afterward, potatoes—grown on the west side of Pacific Avenue from Church Street to the beach—had become the most lucrative and jaw-dropping crop. Residents of New Orleans couldn't contain their exuberance when a shipment arrived in March 1852: "Potatoes from Mr. H. Speel, of Santa Cruz, 120 pounds from five vines on a single hill!"[49] The following year, Blackburn's potatoes received glowing accolades at the Crystal Palace Fair in New York: "The Judge sent samples of potatoes of four pounds weight…and received a premium for the finest potatoes ever seen."[50]

The glory days for local spuds ended all too soon. Given the fortunes being made by Blackburn and others, farmers rushed to plant potato fields throughout the county. Concurrent with the glutted market came a potato bug infestation, as described in the *San Francisco Alta* in 1854: "The bulk of the domestic crop were found to be affected by worms."[51] And the *Sacramento Union* bemoaned the thousands of sacks of Santa Cruz potatoes begging for a market.[52]

But the ever-intrepid Blackburn quickly turned his potato patch into an orchard on lower Pacific, eventually boasting two thousand trees. With apples as the primary crop, he produced forty-five varieties "equal to anything of the species in this or any other country." His clients eventually included brokers in China. By 1856, James Williams—another one of the early arrivals—had also planted his thirty downtown acres with apples as well as other fruit trees. And the *Sentinel* added to the list, reporting, "The Orchards of Hiram A. Imus and David Gharkey back of the old Mission are well worth a visit."[53]

A Novel Idea

Growing up as a slave in Tennessee, could London (aka Louden) Nelson have imagined that one day he would own a prime piece of agricultural land in a small frontier township? Like many other pioneers, his life changed dramatically with the discovery of gold in California. Matthew Nelson, a resident of Knoxville, chose two of his nine slaves to travel with him to the mines in 1850: a blacksmith named Marlborough and London, who handled the cooking and domestic chores. Staking a claim in El Dorado County, the trio worked it for several years with some success. Before Matthew Nelson returned home, both Marlborough and London bought their freedom, with the latter choosing to settle in Santa Cruz in 1856.[54]

Sizing up the agricultural scene, he decided to rent a lot on Front Street, behind today's post office, for his market garden. The proprietor, James L. Prewitt, a forty-niner from Alabama, helped London by providing him with a horse and wagon to sell produce door to door. Settling in a small cabin, London ultimately staked his limited fortune on growing a fruit untried by other local farmers. His sandy soil, conveniently located near a spring of water, proved ideal for watermelons, a very popular crop in the mining regions. For the next few years, London drove through town at harvest times, never lacking customers for his melons.

At age sixty, he purchased the prolific three-quarter-acre garden, paying Prewitt $250 for the deed in 1860. Unfortunately, London suffered from terminal lung disease. Consulting his doctor, Asa Rawson, a dedicated abolitionist and the first physician in Santa Cruz, they discussed how best to dispose of his estate. London never had access to school because it was

At Pacific and Front Streets, James Prewitt's livery stable is on the left in front of the two-story Santa Cruz House Hotel. London Nelson's garden and cabin were located behind the two structures in 1860. *Courtesy of MAH.*

The London Nelson Memorial committee gathers in 1953 to honor his contributions. Third from left is Reverend Dennis Franklin of the NAACP and fourth from left is Reverend Dr. William Brent, pastor of the Missionary Baptist Church. *Courtesy of Covello and Covello.*

illegal in his home state to educate a slave. He decided to leave the land to the Santa Cruz schools, a gift deeply appreciated by the community. The *Sentinel* wrote of his passing in May with a front-page obituary, and friends provided a plot at Evergreen.[55] London Nelson was among the cemetery's first half dozen burials, one year before the start of the Civil War.

Cohesion among Pioneers

One of the many forty-niners to settle in Santa Cruz, Uriah Thompson farmed in both downtown Santa Cruz and the Pajaro Valley before deciding on a permanent location between the two areas. But first he sought to win the hand of one of the most capable women in town.

The oldest offspring of Judge Henry and Lucy Imus Rice, Charlotte had arrived in Santa Cruz at age eighteen. By the following year, 1853, she frequently filled in for Lucy, who had five other children, as the proprietress of the family's temperance establishment, Rice's Hotel. Called the "queen of every department under her care," Charlotte's attention to detail included fresh flowers in each room.[56] Though she met dozens of guests coming and going, it took four years for "Mr. Right"—Uriah Thompson—to walk into the hotel lobby.

She became Charlotte Rice Thompson in 1856, and the couple permanently settled on a large farm in Rodeo Gulch. They became dedicated members of the local Society of California Pioneers of Santa Cruz (see Appendix II). Although women composed less than 20 percent of the organization and were eligible only for honorary membership, Charlotte's relatives and friends were among them, including her first cousin Katherine Imus Hunter and Eliza Boston.

Meanwhile, the Thompsons' apple business thrived. "Thompson Cider" was reputedly the sweetest in the county, and Uriah generously shared his creation at the Farmer's Exchange Fair. Beloved for his amiable manner, was he too kind to win his race for county sheriff? Uriah's tireless effort to grow Santa Cruz's fledgling Democratic Party helped elect his close friend, fellow Missourian W.T. Jeter, as district attorney in 1884, the first-ever Democrat to hold the office.

Charlotte and Uriah had four children, one of whom, Frances Minerva, died in infancy. In 1900, their son Henry passed on at age forty-three (see page 65). Just three years later, Uriah, a seemingly vigorous and healthy man,

Left: Forty-niner Uriah Thompson hailed from Cape Giradeau, Missouri, hometown of James Williams. Life in Santa Cruz appealed to many former residents of the Show Me State. *Courtesy of MAH.*

Right: This obelisk, with a traditional Masonic symbol, honors Charlotte Rice Thompson's parents, pioneers Henry and Lucy Imus Rice. *Photo by Gary Neier.*

died of heart failure. The community responded with a funeral procession "a mile in length and one of the largest ever seen in this county."[57] For the next five years—when she was well into her seventies—Charlotte managed the 140-acre Rodeo Gulch orchard and farmland herself. By this time, the male line of her Imus relatives had moved away, but many of the women remained. Charlotte typified the pioneer resilience learned from her grandmother Ruth Imus, and the *Sentinel* had this to say at her passing at age eighty: "One of the finest of women who grew to womanhood in Santa Cruz and resided in Santa Cruz County ever after."[58] Charlotte Rice Thompson was laid to rest in 1916 with her parents, husband and two of her children in the Rice family plot.

From Dairy Farm to Tourist Destination

Born and raised in England, Thomas Pilkington worked as a translator in the Mexican-American War. Upon arriving in Santa Cruz, his fluency in Spanish served him well. He met his bride, Mary Caroline Galbraith, through the Cooper family, her close friends from their shared childhood in Gettysburg, Pennsylvania. Thomas and Mary Caroline's dairy farm on the east side of the San Lorenzo consisted of seventy-five acres, encompassing most of the west side of today's Seabright.

Instrumental in establishing the Congregational church, the couple were among the original twelve members "who united in Christian Fellowship Sunday, September 13, 1857." One of two original deacons, Thomas also served as clerk during the church's construction phase. The Greek Revival structure, completed a year later, captured the attention of architectural writer John Chase: "The building's New England appearance was due to the Massachusetts training of its carpenter and architect John B. Perry."[59] The first of three Congregational church buildings in the city, this location served many worshipers who would later be buried at Evergreen.

Though Thomas Pilkington's commitment to the Congregational church continued until the end of his life in 1888, his role as dairy farmer did not. In 1876, when his beloved Caroline died in a freak buggy accident, he changed his focus. Summer tourists had begun to discover the Seabright area, and Pilkington embraced the potential. He reinvented himself as a developer, first with a tent camp overlooking the beach and then a subdivision to accommodate picturesque beach bungalows. What would best serve the charming seaside community in the long run? That mindset propelled his decision-making and helped preserve the locality's special beauty. As tourism replaced the Pilkington dairy, another operation flourished several miles north.

A Dairy Hub Is Born

Grace Archer, at just seventeen, started a private school in London and continued her teaching career for a decade. When a countryman, having made a modest fortune in California real estate, returned home for a visit, he was smitten with Grace. Miss Archer married Joseph Errington in 1865, and her sophisticated and predictable life changed dramatically.

Congregationalists worshiped at this Greek Revival–style church, located on Church Street, for thirty-two years. *Courtesy of MAH.*

Once the couple arrived in California, Joseph searched for the ideal location to build a dairy business. Deciding on the Scotts Valley ranch of Hiram Scott, Joseph paid $6,750 for 1,140 acres, though a later survey showed he had title to only 470. Bringing in the best cows from Marin County and building state-of-the-art milking barns paid off with high demand for the Erringtons' milk and cheese. Significantly, the enterprising couple paved the way for Scotts Valley to become a thriving dairy hub for nearly a century. Meanwhile, Grace's extreme isolation became more endurable with the births of her first two children, Mamie and <u>Landreth</u>, but she never adjusted to being "surrounded by rattlesnakes."[60] Tragically, after only four years of marriage, Joseph died at age forty-eight, and the bottom fell out of her world.

An exceptional manager, Grace kept the farm productive while simultaneously raising a young child and an infant. In 1873, she married <u>Achilles Hicks</u>, a widower and sawmill owner from Ben Lomond. With her two children, Achilles's son Nathaniel and the three boys the couple had together—Jesse, Percy and George—they became quite a prominent "blended" family. All six children received baptism in the Congregational Church, and the family made the long buggy trip into Santa Cruz every Sunday. Grace surely appreciated the high-quality music at the church, having grown up in a family of musicians with a brother who played in the Duke of Edinburgh's band. Her role evolved from dairy manager into overseeing the farm's extended family. By 1880, it consisted of a dozen members, including her mother, <u>Mary Archer</u>, and relatives of both her late husband and Achilles.

Known as young men destined to make a difference, Percy and <u>Jesse Hicks's</u> popularity followed them from Scotts Valley Elementary School to Santa Cruz High. It even continued when they studied engineering together at University of California–Berkeley. But for the large and lively Jesse, tragedy struck during his senior year. During a pickup game of football at UC, he sustained a broken neck and died the following day. His memorial service in November 1899 packed the Congregational church in Santa Cruz. Mourners included Berkeley's President Wheeler, who delivered a moving eulogy.

The Live Oak Dairy Farm remained intact until 1912, when <u>Grace Errington Hicks</u> sold her one-third share and moved to Santa Cruz, where she passed on in 1929 at age ninety-one. Grace never lost her English refinement and imbued her children with the importance of faith and education. Moreover, she served as vice president of the local suffragists

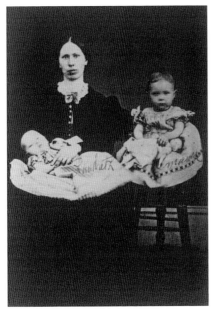 

Left: Grace Archer Errington poses with her first children. Landreth is on her lap with Mamie sitting on a stool. *Courtesy of Scotts Valley Historical Society.*

Right: Jesse and Percy Hicks both pursued degrees in engineering at the University of California–Berkeley. Jesse suffered a fatal accident playing football. *Courtesy of MAH.*

and witnessed the first decade of American women exercising their right to vote. Forty years later, when dairies had all but vanished from Scotts Valley, city leaders wanted to recognize the family's longevity and significant contribution. For whatever reason, Albert Errington, Grace's descendant, declined the city's offer to name the current Siltanen Park Errington Park.

FROM PASTURELAND TO STRAWBERRY FIELDS

A permanent cattle ranch was what Charles Imus had envisioned when he purchased the Potrero, but that dream faded with his death in 1856. Within a decade, his brother Hiram Jr. had transformed the land into an extensive, well-diversified farm. Adding to his orchard of fruit trees, he had twelve thousand hills of strawberries on twelve acres, evidently averaging around 1,800 quarts a week. His frequent delivery of complimentary berries to the *Sentinel* earned high praise: "We have never seen larger or finer berries anywhere, even in the most favorable seasons."[61] During Evergreen's first twenty years, visitors enjoyed the stunning view on the opposite side of Evergreen Street: the Imus groves of pears, plums, apples and apricots, in addition to the strawberry hills. "Nothing of this kind can be found in the state, outside of Santa Cruz County, to surpass it."[62] But the thriving family farm would come to an end when two events happened in close proximity. In the mid-1870s, Hiram passed on, and the Felton–Santa Cruz railroad ran its line through the land.

THE CHINESE MARKET GARDENS

The plethora of "firsts" William Blackburn achieved in Santa Cruz was no doubt possible because of his wife's devoted support. As is often the case with Victorian-era women, Harriet Mead Blackburn also deserves recognition in her own right. She was in her early thirties and the judge fifty-one when their only child, Fredrick Snyder Blackburn, was born, but their immense joy would be short-lived. Beginning in 1863, with the death of her nephew Ruel Kittredge (see page 60), Harriet endured a period of unfathomable loss. The following year, Fredrick, a toddler, died of consumption. Two years later, William Blackburn would also be laid to rest at Evergreen with no heirs to carry on the name. Many aspects of town life had felt his influence, and Harriet as a young widow would now oversee vast amounts of Santa Cruz real estate. Her stewardship was groundbreaking.

The flatland between Mission Hill and the San Lorenzo River had transitioned from a fruit grower's paradise into a bustling business and residential hub by the 1870s. But the extensive Blackburn orchard, adjacent to Neary Lagoon, had not gone the way of developers, thanks to Harriet's vision. She rented the prime acreage west of her orchard to a partnership of local Chinese gardeners. In March 1876, the *Sentinel* reported on their success: "Selling green peas in the streets of Santa Cruz—three pounds for twenty cents—fresh and crisp, from the basket," raised with other "fine vegetables in their gardens."[63]

Another prominent pioneer family followed suit six months later. Judge Rice signed a contract leasing a section of his Branciforte farm for a term of five years to a group of Chinese entrepreneurs. "The Chinese lessee," columnist Ernest Otto recalled, "was only known as Judge Rice and he would drive through the city crying what he had to sell."[64] In fact, the clear early morning call of Chinese peddlers was both expected and appreciated in Santa Cruz. For the first time, locals had several fresh vegetables to choose from along with a variety of berries. The *Sentinel* publicized the success of Rice's tenants "making lots of money this year out of strawberries"[65] of high quality. The judge renewed the lease in 1881 and continued to do so thereafter.

Another well-known widow, Eliza Boston (see page 67), also rented her extensive property to the Chinese. Ernest Otto was effusive: "No garden spot could be prettier, and from sunrise to sunset the industrious Chinese continued their work on the land almost from High to King Street.... The Chinese gardeners also raised choice blackberries, raspberries, and gooseberries. In the creek the Chinese grew special delicacies for themselves, such as a water chestnut bulb much used in preparing Chinese dishes....The Chinese lived in unpainted cabins with...sheds for delivery wagons and horses."[66] Because the Chinese lived on her land, Boston had frequent contact with them. In response to the rising tide of animosity from the "Chinese Must Go" movement, one night she brought several of them into her home on Davis Street. They wanted to know if she was fearful, and she instantly responded, "A woman's tongue and broomstick are a match for any mob."[67]

Persecution did not stop the Chinese market gardeners who, by 1900, were two dozen strong on the west side. Historian Sandy Lydon summarizes their situation: "Only the market gardens offered the kind of economic opportunity which might propel some of the Chinese to the second stage of the immigrant experience, but they were getting older and time was beginning to run out."[68]

Chapter 6

CIVIL WAR AND REMEMBRANCE

A war of words between <u>Dr. Francis Kittredge</u> and Henry Rice ran in the press as the presidential campaign of 1860 drew near. The doctor, who supported Abraham Lincoln, implored the judge to follow his example and renounce the Democratic Party, but Rice, an advocate for peace, refused. When Santa Cruzans learned about the attack on Fort Sumter and the subsequent declaration of war, they gathered together at Rice's Hall on Pacific Avenue. There were disagreements on some issues, but in the end, the audience—which included the doctor and the judge—united to give three cheers for the Union and the Stars and Stripes.

A leading Republican, Albert Brown, undertook to raise a cavalry company of local men, "most of them expert horsemen."[69] The company assembled at the Congregational church, where Reverend Bartlett blessed their banners before they marched to the beach. There, a crowd of citizens cheered when the soldiers boarded a San Francisco–bound steamer, and local ladies distributed hand-sewn haversacks containing needles and thread, fine-tooth combs and crush towels.

The Santa Cruz volunteers, designated as Company L, Second California Cavalry, included Sergeant <u>Asa Anthony</u>, nephew of Elihu, who helped Captain Brown drill the troops. "They go forward cheerfully to defend the rights of their country,"[70] Brown reported. Company L's new home, known as "Camp Alert," just outside the city of San Francisco, had been a racetrack before the war. "The ground is perfectly level," a correspondent observed, "and well adapted to winter quarters. A platform built a foot from the ground, upon which is pitched the company's tents, affords ample protection from the weather."[71] This might have been true in a dry year, but the rainy season of 1861–62 still ranks as one of the worst on record. Unsheltered horses stood dejectedly in the mud, as the men in tents began to suffer the effects of poor sanitation. By early December, six men had already died of typhoid. At the end of the month, the Santa Cruz Company suffered its first casualty when Asa Anthony died of the disease. He was buried at Evergreen, next to the grave of his grandfather, whose name he shared.

Finally receiving marching orders in mid-July 1862, Company L would guard the Overland Trail in Nevada. Before leaving San Francisco, however, the regimental surgeon issued a medical discharge to another Santa Cruzan, Ruel W. Kittredge, the Kittredges' only son. Suffering from consumption, he returned to his parents' home on Beach Hill, where he died seven months later. A year later, Francis and Almira's only daughter, Marietta, age twenty-six and an avid student of music, died of tuberculosis, joining her brother at Evergreen.

Santa Cruzans used Fourth of July festivities in 1863 to support another of their own who had recently been sent home. Although local women raised seventy-two dollars for James Monroe Hecox, his health continued to deteriorate, and he passed on by summer's end. "The third of the Santa Cruz Volunteers who have come home to die, was buried in Evergreen Cemetery." Captain Brown commended him as "a good soldier; patient, uncomplaining and always ready and reliable."[72]

GRAND ARMY OF THE REPUBLIC

Thanks to the efforts of Union veterans, membership in the Grand Army of the Republic (GAR) grew rapidly immediately after the war. Captain Brown, as commander of the Santa Cruz GAR post, invited the public to keep "fresh the remembrance of those who fell gloriously upon the field of battle, as well as those who suffered all the hardship of the march and died in hospitals."[73] On Sunday, May 30, 1869, citizens joined local veterans— some on foot and others in carriages—for the march to Evergreen Cemetery, culminating with the scattering of flowers over soldiers' graves.

Although a similar celebration took place in 1870, it took years for Memorial Day (aka Decoration Day) to become an annual event. The political turmoil of the Reconstruction era and the GAR's staunch support of the increasingly controversial administration of President Grant probably contributed to the declining interest. Before long, the local post quietly disbanded and the public celebrations ceased altogether. When the state legislature made Memorial Day a legal holiday in the late 1870s, the local *Courier-Item* hoped "to see Santa Cruz pause for a day to remember and recount the deeds of valor which preserved the unity of our Republic."[74]

The Union veterans of Santa Cruz agreed. As the town transformed itself into a small city, their number had increased because of the influx of newcomers from the Midwest and East, including many survivors of unbelievably bloody battles. These men, often without families, worried about where they would eventually be interred, as most of the plots at Evergreen were already claimed by pioneers. In 1880, another Memorial Day went without notice, prompting the *Sentinel* to recall the sacrifice of Santa Cruz's "own" and urging appropriate ceremonies to honor them. Within weeks, regrets gave way to action. On August 11, about twenty-five former Union soldiers met to establish a new post, led by Thomas Amner.

Arriving in America from England in 1862, master mechanic Amner enlisted in a Connecticut regiment responsible for protecting Washington, D.C. After the war, he settled in Santa Cruz and owned an iron foundry. Active in the Masonic order and the Episcopal Church, he also became a leader in the local Republican Party, served a term on the city council and

Seen from the hill above Evergreen is a National Guard encampment in the mid-1880s. A decade earlier, the Imuses' extensive orchard covered the land. *Courtesy of MAH.*

Thomas Amner's foundry and machine shop at the foot of Mission Hill specialized in moving parts for the local railroads. *Courtesy of MAH.*

often enjoyed the role of grand marshal for patriotic parades. Members of the GAR post chose Amner as their commander, and in 1882, he led the revival of Memorial Day. A grand procession of veterans and fellow citizens proudly marched first to Evergreen and then other local cemeteries. "We shall owe much to the Grand Army of the Republic," A.A. Taylor of the *Courier Item* editorialized, "if it maintains the observance of this day."[75]

Amner and his wife, Georgie, celebrated their crystal anniversary in January 1885, surrounded by friends and their five children. Weeks later, on Valentine's Day, Thomas Amner went to the yard behind his foundry shop, evidently to shoot gophers. Minutes later, the gun went off prematurely, killing him. He was forty-four years old.

Civic organizations coalesced to honor their fallen leader. Although the GAR had secured a 1,200-foot plot adjacent to the Masonic section at Evergreen, Mrs. Amner chose to have her husband interred in the family plot. Nonetheless, Memorial Day held special significance for local Grand Army of the Republic members. "For the first time our memorial service will be held at a cemetery especially our own and made doubly dear by being the last resting place of our beloved Post Commander."[76] Mourners stood in awe, gazing at the elaborate floral décor, including scarlet geraniums. For Georgie Amner, the tragedy only worsened. Within the year, her infant son Edgar passed on, joining his father at Evergreen.

Chapter 7

SANTA CRUZ SINGS

INDIGENOUS PEOPLE AND THE MISSION'S MUSIC

On September 25, 1891, Catholics and Protestants joined in a special centennial commemoration of the founding of the Santa Cruz Mission. The diverse and colorful procession drew quite a crowd who watched dozens of dignitaries fill the seats on the grandstand. The honorees included Lorenzo Asisara, a seventy-two-year-old Ohlone born at the mission and the former leader of the Catholic church choir.

In 1835, Governor José Figueroa invited the teenage Lorenzo to Monterey, where he learned to play the clarinet from Sergeant Rafael Estrada. When Lorenzo later returned to the Santa Cruz Mission, Padre Antonio Real enabled him to master Spanish. With this unique skill set, he became the director of the choir—consisting primarily of native men—a role that abruptly ended when the original adobe church collapsed in 1857. Longtime parish priest Joaquín Adam recalled hearing Lorenzo and a couple of his friends. "They sang for me on Holy Thursday, Good Friday and Holy Saturday and it was a treat to hear them."[77] The versatile musicians also played for dances and local festivities.

Lorenzo, who did not speak at the 1891 centennial, did provide well-articulated oral histories. What a contrast they were from the words of the celebration's keynote speaker. "At the very beginning," the visiting priest told the audience, "the Indians came from all directions to be taught. They were received with kindness and affection. The acorns on which the

Early days of the Santa Cruz Mission—a postcard published by Edward Mitchell—was adapted from the 1870s painting by Leon Trousset. *Courtesy of Online Archive of California.*

Indians had lived were abandoned to the swine and the forests forsaken for more civilized abodes."[78]

With his vivid memory, buttressed by the oral tradition of his people, Lorenzo offered two detailed accounts in 1877 and 1890 of the mission period. He recalled the words of his Ohlone father: "To capture the wild Indian, first were taken the children, and then the parents followed. The padres would erect a hut and light the candles to say Mass and the Indians, attracted by the light—thinking they were stars—would approach, and soon be taken." From these stories he concluded that "the Spanish priests were very cruel with the Indians: they mistreated them a lot, they kept them poorly fed, ill clothed, and they made them work like slaves. The priests did not practice what they preached at the pulpit." Lorenzo did point out that he had not been personally subjected to severe treatment.[79]

A few years after the centennial, Lorenzo died at the county hospital; the date remains a mystery since his passing went unrecorded. Prior to his death, according to his translator friend E.L. Williams, Lorenzo had abandoned the Catholic faith and returned to the religion of his people and the Asisara family. According to Williams and to Charles Herber, the cemetery sexton during that time, Lorenzo's remains were interred in the Potters' Field at Evergreen.[80]

LIFE OF THE LOCAL STAR

When eighty Soquel schoolchildren performed a concert for the community in 1866, Judge Henry Rice's nine-year-old grandson and namesake, Henry Thompson, stole the show with his rendition of "Our American Flag." Who knew the precocious boy would make an enduring mark on the music culture of the county! Young Henry, who grew up on his family's Rodeo Gulch ranch, attended St. Augustine's College in Benicia, assuming he would become a lawyer. Heavily influenced by Judge Rice, he took a position in the secretary of state's office but soon found the law distasteful. Redefining his future, Henry committed to developing his basso voice, described by a music critic as "rare in power and rich in tone."[81]

At age twenty-five, he headed for Milan to study opera with the best in the business, but not before his going-away party at the Santa Cruz Opera House. The occasion drew an appreciative crowd, including his close friend Frank Heath, an aspiring landscape painter. As a goodbye gift, Heath presented Henry with an oil painting of the West Cliff Drive lighthouse, prompting a reporter's effusive response: "Frank's pictures, in time, will perhaps secure a European reputation."[82]

Acclimating quickly to Italian customs, Henry basked in the positive reviews from seasoned opera critics, writing to the *Sentinel* in the early 1880s, "I acquired a considerable reputation as De Tomasso in Italy, and you know, in the theatrical or operatic business, there's a good deal in a name, therefore if I had called myself Henry Thompson I might not have so readily secured an engagement."[83] With a local following, reporters often referred to him as Enrico de Tomasso, but those who knew him well preferred "Our Henry."

But along with positive reviews came pitfalls, such as the broken bones he sustained when a Milan stage collapsed. After close to four years abroad, he returned to American soil, giving performances in New York, Philadelphia and Chicago, yet the variety of venues hardly offset his frustrations. Compared with the capitals of Europe, America's major cities only meagerly supported classic opera. To pay the bills, Henry signed on with various light opera companies, including the quite popular Haverly Minstrels in 1887. He played a range of roles, sometimes in blackface. Roving from one metropolitan area to another, he amassed more than twenty thousand miles, proclaiming his love for the bohemian life.

When he returned to Santa Cruz with the Haverly Minstrels show in the summer of 1899, his priorities included singing at the 1899 funeral of Mary Case. Was the occasion a poignant reminder of the Evergreen Cemetery community, where seven of his Imus relatives were already interred, as well as his sister Frances? Henry elected to stay home. Whether smitten or just intrigued, he focused his attention on music teacher Lottie Dame, acclaimed for her contributions to the Congregational church choir.

Locals had kept tabs on Enrico's peripatetic career thanks to his engaging letters to the *Sentinel*; fans now had the thrill of attending live performances. One at the Unity Church in 1890 prompted a reporter's glowing account: "Signor Enrico De Tomasso's singing was heartily encored and his voice reverberated from one end of the church to the other."[84] Henry had found his niche promoting a vibrant music culture in Santa Cruz. Generous to a fault, he gladly gave benefit concerts for causes he believed in, including several for the county Democratic Party. Reconnecting with his friend from a decade earlier, music teacher and tenor Rollin Case, the men produced duets, formed a quartet with two local women and dreamed of sponsoring a musical convention. In a flurry of activity, Enrico and Lottie performed together in comic operas and philharmonic concerts at the popular Opera House. The on- and off-stage courtship solidified, drawing considerable local interest.

The elegant Santa Cruz Opera House opened in November 1877. Though rarely hosting operas, it drew crowds for wrestling matches, magic shows, theatrical productions and concerts by Henry Thompson and other local musicians. *Courtesy of MAH.*

Imagine having a guest list of five hundred, and then eight hundred people show up. Such was the Thompson wedding in June 1892, when hundreds of uninvited well-wishers tried to crowd into Calvary Episcopal Church. "The rush was so great that several ladies fainted." Nonetheless, it would "always rank among the most elaborate and pretty weddings ever seen in this city."[85] Soon after, Enrico became Calvary's choir director, where he, Lottie and Rollin performed together. The community cherished the couple's abilities and frequent benefits for local churches and causes. Yet the city's population—around 5,500—offered only so much opportunity for musicians. The husband-and-wife team moved to Sacramento, where Enrico flourished with plenty of students. Those halcyon days would be short-lived; Enrico's deteriorating health brought them back to Santa Cruz in 1897.

Convalescing in Lottie's family home, Beach Hill's Carmelita Cottages, Enrico revived his lifelong friendship with neighbor Frank Heath. Despite Enrico's battle with consumption, his passion for promoting musical organizations and training the young men's chorus remained irrepressible to the end. He died at age forty-three where he was born—at the home of his parents, Uriah and Charlotte Thompson. In August 1900, the *Sentinel* reported, "About the longest funeral procession ever seen on Pacific Avenue was that of Henry Thompson. Henry was a universal favorite with all classes of people."[86] His grandest plans for music in Santa Cruz never had time to fully materialize, but his passionate dedication touched the lives of many aspiring vocalists and raised music appreciation to a new level.[87]

THE MUSIC OF CALVARY: A 155-YEAR COMMITMENT

Eliza Boston's (née Bull) background—raised in New York State by a cultured family with strong abolitionist values—helps explain the mindset she brought to her adopted home of Santa Cruz. She arrived in 1861 at age twenty-nine, a decade beyond suitable marriage age in the Victorian era. Nonetheless, she soon wed local businessman Joseph Boston, part owner of a tannery.[88] The couple shared an unwavering devotion to their Episcopalian faith, and when Eliza donated land to provide a permanent home for the peripatetic parish, Joseph gave his wholehearted support.

Literally in the center of town—532 Center Street—Calvary Episcopal today is the oldest church building in the city. An unmistakable cathedral-like feel owes much to the original nine-foot-high stained-glass windows the

Eliza Boston's New York education and values helped shape the culture of the town. A pillar of the Episcopal Church, her faith characterized a long and productive life. *Courtesy of Covello and Covello.*

Rollin Case (*top row, third from right*), best known as a vocalist and music teacher, also enjoyed performing with the popular Hastings band. *Courtesy of MAH.*

Bostons imported from the East Coast. As a church leader, Eliza insisted on the highest standards for Protestant music, and Joseph donated a melodeon. The quality of the ensemble, which included Rollin Case, beckoned folks to Anglican services. With considerable popularity as a vocalist, music director and teacher, Case charged fifty cents for public concerts. But even while playing in Professor George Hasting's band, he always found time for the Calvary choir.

A natural networker, Eliza joined the town's first female social club. Amid the tightknit circle of twelve was Mary Perry Jordan, wife of Albion. The club, founded in 1859, adhered to a strict set of rules for their monthly meetings, such as who would be permitted to invite guests and precisely what refreshments could be served: bread, butter, pickles, one kind of cold meat, cake, coffee and tea.

Such an auspicious beginning as a promoter of culture and refinement in the rough-hewn West contrasted sharply with the heart-rending tragedy that followed. By her mid-forties, Eliza had lost their only son, William Boston (age six), in a horrific freak accident. Subsequently, Joseph took his own life, and her brother Thomas died from the effects of insanity. Yet amid the years of adversity, she raised three daughters who lived meaningful lives and became even more devoted to her church and serving those around her. At the height of the "Chinese Must Go" movement, Eliza took bold steps to support the Chinese market gardeners who rented her land.

Eliza Bull Boston's legacy—in addition to establishing the Episcopal church—includes her many writings and speeches often given to celebrate the anniversaries of other churches in addition to her own. One talk—given in her seventies—focused on the pioneer period: "Those were strenuous times and they made us women who did and dared. And I don't think we used our liberty wrongly either. We loved each other a great deal in those days, but I've since found out that if you want to love your neighbor as yourself, you had better not get too close to him."[89]

With unshakeable faith and resilience, Eliza inspired women of her era to stand up and speak out for what they believed in. As a tireless advocate for Calvary's music program, she would surely rejoice that the special quality continues. In July 2018, the church purchased the Schoenstein Opus 84 (1981) pipe organ. The fine instrument pairs well with the church's consistently strong choral music, as well as with the special concerts offered to the public in all seasons.

Chapter 8

CREATIVE HUB

A Nineteenth-Century Feminist

Belle (Lovina Isabel) Smith, born in Farmington, Utah, in 1854, became Mrs. William Harrell at age sixteen. Belle's beauty and talent seemed to dazzle men, and her theatrical personal life—three marriages and evidently one broken engagement—kept her followers on the edges of their seats. Her search for adventure, exceptional for a Victorian woman, gave her special access to stories that illuminated Santa Cruz history in the post–Civil War era. As a journalist, she used the surname of her second husband in her byline, <u>Belle Dormer</u>.

Thrilling the community, local leader William T. Jeter made possible the first-ever visit by a president to Santa Cruz in May 1891. Benjamin Harrison, the champion of the Forest Preserve Act, insisted on visiting Felton Big Trees with absolutely no media fanfare. But when reporters mobbed his grand procession through Santa Cruz, no one produced a more charming account than Belle, having taken notes from her balcony seat at the Pacific Ocean House:

> *The carriage containing the president was drawn by four white horses, and was completely covered with the most choice and beautiful flowers [as were]…the fourteen other carriages. Pacific Avenue looked like a bridle path through a forest of waving palm. Every woman and child and many*

White-haired President Harrison rides in a carriage through town, escorted by fellow members of the Grand Army of the Republic. He relished the warmth of Santa Cruzans during his historic 1891 visit. *Courtesy of MAH.*

Belle Smith Dormer insisted on overcoming limitations faced by Victorian-era women. In Santa Cruz, she distinguished herself as a journalist and poet. *Courtesy of MAH.*

men held armfuls of flowers which they threw before the presidential party. President Harrison's…face is clear cut, and far more genteel and refined-looking than any portrait I have ever seen of him. He said…in no place had his heart gone out to the people with a more kindly feeling than in the little flower-strewn town of Santa Cruz.…He bowed kindly to the right and left and seemed to take great interest in the decorations and preparations.… From the Pacific Ocean House the party drove to the narrow-gauge depot… and the president stood on the back platform of the car…leaving behind him wagon-loads of perfumed, withering flowers and hundreds of people who would die happy because they had seen a real live president.[90]

Four years later, Belle meticulously covered the momentous San Francisco convention in support of women's suffrage in California. Keynote speaker Susan B. Anthony—having stayed in Santa Cruz years earlier to promote the cause and to visit her cousin, prominent businessman Elihu Anthony—enjoyed a strong local following. From Belle's pen came an extensive assessment of the convention: "Loud hands clapping interrupted the flow of eloquence from the lips of Miss Anthony, and the waving handkerchiefs in the crowded seats, packed aisles, and jammed galleries looked like myriad mammoth flakes of purest snow."[91]

Belle's fascination with the early pioneer period prompted her unique interview of Maria Castro Majors, age seventy-eight, whose family played a significant role in Santa Cruz both before and during the state's transition from Mexican to American rule. The detailed article, "Once Heiress to a Vast California Domain Who Is Now Supported by Charity," recounts how a highly revered, generous family lost their vast and valuable land because, in Maria's words, "the Americanos came like hungry wolves."[92]

Though enamored with the Central Coast, Belle's wanderlust could not be contained. Her eye was on the Klondike, where gold rush fever had taken hold a few years before. She packed up her two young sons, who were half brothers, in the late 1890s, and off they went to Alaska. Five years later, she married Daniel McCarthy while she was still legally married to Dormer, her second husband. According to the allegations, he'd deserted her. Decades later, the media summarized Belle's life in the remote wilderness: "She found no precious metal, but uncovered rich human experiences… ran a boarding house, wrote for the first paper published in Nome, took her turn with dog teams and suffered all the privations and hardships of that wild country."[93]

After a life of many uncommon achievements, including being a skilled deer hunter, Belle Dormer eventually returned permanently to Santa Cruz and devoted herself to writing—mostly poetry—for the *Santa Cruz Sentinel*. She passed on in December 1937, and two years later, her older son, Chauncey Harrell, a miner by profession, joined her at Evergreen. Harrell had delighted locals by walking in the Armistice Day Parade with his Alaskan malamute pulling a wagon filled with her six puppies. What a fitting reminder of Belle—her love for Alaska, animals and the ability to thrill an audience with the unexpected.

RENOWNED ARTISTS

"Flourishing" best describes most local churches in 1866, when Lucien and Jane Edwards Heath moved to Santa Cruz from Oregon and immediately joined the Congregationalists. In fact, the Protestant fervor of the late nineteenth century provides essential context for the lives of two renowned artists: the Heaths' son <u>Frank</u> and his eventual wife, <u>Lillian Dake Heath</u>.

Lucien Heath's hardware store, in the heart of Pacific Avenue, attracted a steady stream of customers. Garnering a stellar reputation, he became president of the Santa Cruz County Bank and served two terms in the state legislature. Meanwhile, Frank pursued his singular passion studying at the San Francisco School of Design under the tutelage of Raymond Daubs Yelland, an acclaimed Northern California artist. Yelland's familiarity with transcendentalism and appreciation of the spiritual quality in California landscapes resonated with the young Heath. After finishing art school and enjoying a few years teaching in San Francisco, Frank spent several years exploring his prospects in Los Angeles and San Diego. Though his art was well received, he concluded that no other location could compare with the natural beauty of Santa Cruz.

Delighted to be home, he became officially baptized in the Congregational Church and served as a devoted deacon during much of the 1890s. But his former student and chosen bride, Lillian Dake, had deep roots in the Methodist Church, giving talks on such topics as "The Way of the Cross." Not only did she succeed in winning Frank over to her faith, but she also inspired him to become a Methodist lay preacher who served whenever called. The couple effortlessly blended their faith and art, celebrating God's creation with paintings of Northern California's scenic views. As Frank's reputation spread well beyond California, he captured the attention of internationally renowned evangelist Dwight Moody. Visiting the Heaths' stunningly appointed Beach Hill home and studio in 1899, Moody was taken with the quality of Frank's work and returned home to Chicago with three Frank Heath originals.

The Heaths' commitment to creating an "art-oriented" community may well be unparalleled in the city's history. As noted by *Sentinel* writer Margaret Koch, "Art had not gotten much notice until Frank Heath came on the scene."[94] In 1897, Frank organized plein-air artists into the Jolly Daubers, and their travels between the forest giants and the Pacific epitomized the Southern Pacific Railroad's local slogan: "From the Redwoods to the Sea."

The couple had been married only a few years when tragedy struck, precipitating a new focus for their calling. In 1900, Frank lost two cherished friends: Raymond Yelland, his mentor both during and after art school, and vocalist Henry Thompson, his friend since boyhood and neighbor on Beach Hill. Where would he go for solace? To the Santa Cruz Mountains, it turns out, a place in which he and Lillian could eventually merge their

Frank and Lillian Heath pose in their Beach Hill studio, where he demonstrates brushwork on the canvas. *Courtesy of MAH.*

Frank Heath captured the pastoral beauty surrounding turn-of-the-century Santa Cruz and the San Lorenzo River. This oil painting is on permanent display at the Santa Cruz Public Library. *Photo by Joe Michalak.*

art and spiritual commitment in a new venue. They purchased a second home with an art studio on the meandering Marshall Creek in Ben Lomond, surrounded by towering redwoods. A decade later, spending considerable time at Mount Hermon, the first Christian conference center in the West, the couple inspired the lives of audiences from all over the country.

In the sylvan surroundings, Frank offered a lecture series on "The Mission of Art." He enjoyed quoting Anthony van Dyck, the great Flemish painter, to underscore the true purpose of artistic expression: "To interpret hidden beauty, to reveal unknown truths, to translate hidden language."[95] In 1910, thanks to Frank's efforts, the Mount Hermon Art Studio—an entire building adjacent to the main auditorium—opened to the public. There Frank guided the conference center's summer guests in oil painting while Lillian taught specialized crafts: tapestry weaving and leather tooling.

All the while, the couple continued their commitment to causes in Santa Cruz. Frank, a member of the Methodists' building committee, stood in awe at the dedication of the new church in 1915. All eyes were on the rose window given by Lillian in memory of her stepfather, Judge William Storey, and her mother, Eliza Dufour Storey. The stained glass depicts Jesus in the garden of Gethsemane. Today, it is a central, albeit lofty, feature of the Methodist church at 250 California Street.

Frank, together with marine artist Margaret Rogers, transformed the adventurous Jolly Daubers into the Santa Cruz Art League. As the organization's first president in 1919, he agreed with Rogers that the Seabright Crafts Society building, donated to the city by Susan Tyrell, was the right venue for exhibitions as well as for artists supporting one another.

Admirers of Heath's work came from far and wide, and his one-man show at Mount Hermon's Zayante Inn in 1921 was no exception. The inn and surrounding cottages burned to the ground in April of that year, but Frank never learned of the catastrophic loss. Lillian couldn't bear for her husband to know; he passed on from cancer a few days later.

No family at Evergreen is so uniquely enshrined as the Heaths. Frank joined four relatives in the family's well-secured vault just across the Glory Path walkway from Henry Thompson. The artist's own words provide a fitting epitaph: "Christian people should be above all things unselfish and patriotic, and their lives should be moved by the mighty principle to do right without regard to party politics."[96] The Santa Cruz Art League Frank Heath so selflessly inspired continues to thrive today, a century later.

AN ARTIST IN HER OWN RIGHT

Lillian Dake, as a single woman studying in New York and Chicago in the 1890s, would most likely have come in contact with the work of Berthe Morrisot, one of the only recognized American women artists of the era. By that time, Morrisot had committed to impressionist landscapes, while Heath was a self-described realist. What the two artists did have in common was their delicacy of stroke.

Prior to her marriage, Lillian taught classes in oil painting as well as the decorating of fine china at a price of one dollar per class. As Mrs. Frank Heath, her artistic versatility blossomed. Watercolor became her new medium, but she also expanded her repertoire of decorative arts to include leather modeling with intricate, true-to-life designs on everything from opera bags to book covers. In 1914, the Women's Exchange Exhibition featured Lillian's watercolor renditions of familiar Santa Cruz locations such as De LaVeaga Park, California Redwood Park (Big Basin), Twin Lakes and the San Lorenzo River.

After Frank's death, she continued as a dedicated artist, remaining in their Beach Hill home within easy walking distance of the Art League,

Right: Lillian Heath's still-life oil painting is part of the carefully preserved collection of Heath paintings at the Santa Cruz Methodist Church. *Photo by Gary Neier.*

Below: Watercolor became Lillian Heath's preferred medium after her marriage. This rendering of Natural Bridges reflects her keen interest in iconic local landmarks. *Judith Steen Collection.*

which burgeoned as a cultural center. The Santa Cruz Women's Club, of which she was an active member, celebrated Lillian's work in April 1954 in a remarkably wide-ranging exhibition: watercolors, miniature portraits on fine bone china and leather tooling.

Her devoted membership in the Methodist Church began as a preteen and lasted eighty-four years, until her passing at age ninety-seven in 1961. Decades earlier, Lillian had donated several of Frank's landscapes to the church, a collection still cherished by the Methodist congregation. Today, his huge, mural-size painting of Point Lobos presides over the congregation's community room. Pastor Jay Pierce eagerly points out how the masterpiece draws observers into the breaking waves and captures "the power of nature to reveal God in our midst."

THE GRANDER VIEW

From upstate New York, Nelson Taylor came to California for the gold rush, but after several months with no success, he left the mines "in disgust."[97] He began life in Santa Cruz as one of the original Congregationalists who first met informally at the Imus family's grove in July 1851. When the church incorporated, he became a deacon and then served as the clerk for nearly thirty years. Simultaneously, he served as the county assessor for five terms beginning in 1862 and traversed the entire county on horseback. When his ambitious relative arrived in the mid-1870s, Nelson was probably instrumental in helping him find an idyllic piece of land on Mission Street.

In his mid-twenties and barely five feet tall, Arthur A. Taylor and his bride, Mary Prescott Taylor, left Elmira, New York, where he had enjoyed an acquaintance with Mark Twain. They were enthralled by the natural beauty of Santa Cruz. The couple's home—where they lived for nearly fifty years—offered spectacular views of both the mountains and the bay, and today, it serves as part of the Santa Cruz High School campus. Perhaps the panoramic view inspired Taylor's vision for Santa Cruz, which may well be unparalleled during the post–Civil War era.

By the late 1870s, when Santa Cruz had almost reached four thousand residents, newcomer Taylor saw enormous potential. He consolidated small local newspapers and soon launched his own daily paper, the *Santa Cruz Surf*, in direct competition with the well-established *Santa Cruz Sentinel*. Feisty, righteous and irreverent, Democrat Taylor became an unrelenting champion of the causes he believed in. A lover of beauty and culture, he

Left: Publisher, writer and preservationist A.A. Taylor poses at his desk at the *Santa Cruz Surf*. *Courtesy of MAH*.

Below: The *Santa Cruz Surf* occupied the upstairs of this building on Pacific Avenue, formerly the site of the Arcan family home and store. *Courtesy of Covello and Covello*.

used the *Surf* to promote the arts and women's organizations committed to beautifying the town. His reporters' reviews of theater performances and art exhibitions included compelling details not available elsewhere.

Based on his first three decades in Santa Cruz—which included public feuds with *Sentinel* newspaper owner and Republican Duncan McPherson— one might expect the provocateur to become an irascible curmudgeon later in life. In fact, his evolution took a quite different path. Great landscape artists capture the natural world's ineffable qualities; in the case of Taylor, the incomparable Santa Cruz mountain redwoods captured him. He spent the final chapter of his life as a tireless preservationist.

Taylor advocated for state ownership of Big Basin in the early 1890s, years before Santa Cruzans convinced San Jose and other Bay Area communities to join the effort to create California's oldest state park. From the day of the park's opening in June 1904, he maintained a steadfast stewardship to achieve proper park management and greater public access. This diligence earned him a position as a state parks commissioner in 1911. The following year, his book, *California Redwood Park*, offered a florid recounting of the park's creation. In contrast to other male writers of his time and beyond, Taylor gave women the credit due them. Moreover, he dedicated the work to philanthropist Phoebe Apperson Hearst, an early and influential advocate.

Meanwhile, his wife, Mary, who had assisted him at the *Surf* during its early years, had found a special cause. Although she had joined women's organizations at the Methodist church and later at the Universalist church, her passion, as it turned out, was the Women's Aid Society. During her dedicated service as a society director, she was considered "a leading spirit" in attending to Santa Cruz residents in need.

It was the spring of 1917 when thousands of local men between the ages of twenty-one and forty-five registered for service. Amid this all-absorbing focus on the Great War, Taylor opined that the city was in chronic disrepair. What he did about it—declaring his eleventh-hour candidacy for mayor— stunned the community. Negative ads called him both a pessimist and a dreamer. Taylor insisted he had no interest in the job but "someone has got to be willing to make a sacrifice if Santa Cruz is [to be] lifted out of the slough into which it has fallen."[98] His new role as mayor (1917–19) required him to give up his cherished position on the State Parks Commission, where he served as secretary, but not before completing his signature work. Due to Taylor's foresight, the governor signed into law a $150,000 appropriation over five years for the purchase of private land immediately adjacent to Big Basin. The small man with big dreams set in motion a process for land acquisition to

The local movement to save Big Basin united A.A. Taylor and his arch-rival, Duncan McPherson of the *Sentinel*. Andrew P. Hill photographed an expedition of park advocates in 1900, with McPherson fifth from left. *Courtesy of MAH.*

permanently protect the pristine ecosystem, which today at eighteen thousand acres is more than four times the size of the original purchase.

A.A. Taylor, as he was known to many, passed on in August 1923; just four months later, Mary joined him at Evergreen. On the second anniversary of his death, longtime friend William T. Jeter chaired the commemorative event. With hundreds gathered at the cemetery, Jeter read from the memorial plaque donated by the community: "For forty years a leader in initiative, thought and action for the public welfare, he rests here in the place of his choice under the shadows of the trees and hills he loved."[99]

PERFORMING ARTS

Guysbert Bogert Vroom (GBV) "Alphabet" DeLamater said farewell to Indiana in 1850 to cross the plains with a small group of men, which included his close friend "Charley" Crocker. On a night when the travelers camped near the Humboldt River, GBV spied an Indian and quietly called for Charley's help. The two men circled in, rifles cocked, only to discover their "Indian" was in fact just a bush. Years later, GBV turned down Crocker's offer to join him, along with Hopkins, Huntington and Stanford, in their epic transcontinental railroad enterprise. Evidently, GBV had reservations about the Big Four's process for land acquisitions.[100]

Left: Former miner Ah Hoon accompanied the DeLamaters when they moved from the gold country town of Michigan Bar. In Santa Cruz, he lived with the family as their cook. *Courtesy of Nancy Kilfoyl Campeau.*

Below: The DeLamater Eastlake-style house, including Swiss chalet trim, is seen here with its original three-story tower. It remained in the family for more than sixty years. *Courtesy of Nancy Kilfoyl Campeau.*

Alphabet, the name given GBV by locals, arrived in Santa Cruz in 1868 from Michigan Bar, a wealthy mining camp on the American River. Chinese servants were common in mining towns, and Alphabet brought with him Ah Hoon, who "was like one of the family." Evidently, DeLamater and his friend Charley shared a mutual respect for the Chinese, as evidenced by Crocker giving public credit to the Chinese laborers for early completion of the Pacific Railway in 1869.

Once in Santa Cruz, Alphabet and his wife, Eliza Cope DeLamater, joined the Congregational Church and eagerly served in much-needed roles. His considerable experience selling dry goods in both Volcano and Michigan Bar led him to buy a lot on Pacific Avenue and construct a two-story brick building many considered the finest structure in town. DeLamater Dry Goods advertised groceries, cookware, hardware and clothing for all manner of men and boys, while the upstairs hall became a venue for theatrical productions and the meeting space for groups, most often his church. Gaining overnight name recognition, Alphabet became mayor in 1871 and used his one term to promote all aspects of Santa Cruz.

At the Evergreen family plot, he and Eliza reinterred their daughter, Maria Catalina, who died in Michigan Bar. Because easily accessible plots had already been spoken for, Alphabet purchased one straight up a hillside, next to the Heaths' vault. The DeLamater burial site, even today, boasts the most consistent sunshine in a notoriously shady cemetery. The symbolism is noteworthy: Eliza and GBV's daughter Grace, born in 1873, would become a shining light for the arts in Santa Cruz. But due to foul play, the teenage Grace saw her father only intermittently.

In the 1880s, Alphabet used proceeds from a life insurance policy to build the family's Eastlake-style family home on Ocean View Avenue. According to the *Surf*:

> *Some malicious minded persons circulated the report that he was withdrawing money from his business for the home-building and certain creditors made sudden demands for payment which could not be met immediately. Mr. DeLamater was high minded, sensitive and the soul of honor, and instead of asking for any extensions or concessions he sold his* [downtown] *property at a ruinous sacrifice, paying every dollar of his indebtedness, and retired from business. Soon afterwards he entered the supply department of the Southern Pacific, and although the family home has been retained here, his citizenship was transferred to San Francisco to the distinct loss of Santa Cruz.*[101]

Grace DeLamater (*left*) plays the romantic lead as Cinderella's prince. Her willingness to tackle male roles was groundbreaking. *Courtesy of Nancy Kilfoyl Campeau.*

Remaining in Santa Cruz, stalwart Eliza single-handedly managed Ocean View and other rental properties while supporting Grace's remarkable talent. From an early age, she excelled as a contralto, often accompanying performers Henry and Lottie Thompson. As a sought-after singer, Grace dreamed of pursuing a big-city career, but GBV put the kibosh on that idea. As Grace resolved to bloom where she was planted, Santa Cruzans gladly welcomed her to the stage. Grace stole the show during multiple performances of *Cinderella* in 1890, playing a man's role—Prince Amour—flawlessly. That settled it. To supplement her teaching degree from San Jose Normal School, she earned a credential from the California School of Oratory and Elocution. Now fully equipped, she would coach young drama students.

Eliza resolved to stay at Ocean View after GBV DeLamater passed on in 1896. A few years later, when Grace married William Williamson, a court reporter, Eliza invited the newlyweds to move in. With the responsibilities of a full-time wife and mother to daughters Edith and Jean, Grace only performed with the Congregational choir under the direction of Professor George Hastings.

Grace's dear friend Della Pierce Perry, another devoted Congregationalist, also loved classical theater. A local teacher during the 1870s and hailing from New England, Della would defy the Victorian stereotype that women were not smart enough to understand Shakespeare. In 1903, she founded a club focused on English literature and a few years later transformed it into the Friday Shakespeare Club. The dozen dedicated members studied at least two of the Bard of Avon's plays each season. By 1924, with twenty members and a full waiting list, Grace awed them with her rendition of Shylock in *The Merchant of Venice*. Today, the Friday Shakespeare Club continues with meetings at the Peace United Church on High Street.

Mrs. Perry's bold initiative—starting an all-female Shakespeare Club—galvanized Grace. In 1907, she and two friends founded the Santa Cruz Women's Club, dedicated to the performing arts, music, history and landmarks. Honoring the club's golden jubilee in 1957, Grace received recognition as the only surviving founder.

Widowed at the age of forty and with her daughters raised, Grace used her newfound freedom to pursue her passion. Under her tutelage, members of the Santa Cruz High School Drama Club learned Shakespeare and other playwrights in depth. When she coached ZaSu Pitts in the lead role of *Fanchon the Cricket*, it would be the local star's final performance before beginning a brilliant Hollywood career. According to the *Santa Cruz News*,

Passionate about classic theater, Grace Delamater Williamson often performed with the Santa Cruz Shakespeare Club. She received rave reviews for her portrayal of Shylock from *The Merchant of Venice. Courtesy of Nancy Kilfoyl Campeau.*

"All credit is due to Grace Williamson, their director."[102] Grace held students to high standards, and some of the less dedicated thespians winced.

Grace's patriotism shone forth during the Great War, when she walked door to door throughout the city asking friends and strangers alike to buy war bonds. Santa Cruz had one of Northern California's most successful campaigns. When the war ended, Grace signed on for a job at the Boardwalk's Ballroom Casino, where her brother-in-law James Williamson had rescued the failing operation and helped found the Seaside Company. She needed steady income, and the job of ensuring decorum and "respectable behavior" among the ballroom dancers suited her.

When the Depression engulfed Santa Cruz, Grace turned the attic of her Ocean View home into a ballroom dance venue. There she could earn an adequate income while encouraging adult dancers. In addition to her commitment to the performing arts, Grace's abiding support for Evergreen and the maintenance of the family plot is a commitment carried on today by her granddaughter Nancy Kilfoyl Campeau. (See page 112.)

Chapter 9

CHINESE BURIAL GROUND

Funerals with Special Significance

<u>Wong Kee</u>, a successful businessman in Chinatown, served as its unofficial mayor as early as the 1870s. In addition, he enjoyed considerable influence as master of the rapidly growing local chapter of the Chinese Freemasons, the Chee Kong Tong Society. Throughout California, the organization emulated its American counterpart—the Masons—by offering death benefits to members. The state law imposing a fee on disinterment had made it difficult if not impossible for most Chinese to honor their tradition of sending bones back to China. This travesty gave the Chee Kong Tong Society a vital role: initiates were assured their passing would include a funeral and a temporary resting place until circumstances made possible the burial at one's ancestral birthplace.

A burial in 1884—though not the first Chinese interment at Evergreen—provided a unique challenge for Wong Kee. Seventeen-year-old <u>Lou Sing</u>, a Freemason and the cook at the Kloss Ranch on Vine Hill, was found dead at his workplace. The newspaper accounts claimed the well-liked teenager committed suicide following "trouble with white men."[103] The coroner found quantities of strychnine in Lou Sing's stomach and also noted that his neck had been broken. Believing it was murder, society members looked to Wong Kee, who delayed the funeral to consult the Six Companies, advocates for the Chinese headquartered in San Francisco. Within days, an advertisement signed by the Chinese Six Companies appeared in the local paper:

We would like to ask…how could Lou Sing break his neck after he took poison? We say that he was hung after he was leaving the stable with his hands tied behind his back.…We have a witness to the whole proceeding, and will bring him forth when necessary. He says that…a man took Lou Sing by the back of the neck and forced poison into his mouth.…We intend to sift this case to the very bottom.[104]

Lou Sing, a boy with no prominence or money who was learning English at the Congregational Mission, had a magnificent funeral. Wong Kee made sure of it. Chinese Freemasons served as pallbearers, flying their society flag at the front of the procession to Evergreen. The men wore red badges on their customary white garments to indicate murder and set off an abundance of firecrackers that day, far more than usual. According to history professor Sandy Lydon, "Though Lou Sing's murderer was never brought to justice, the Santa Cruz Chinese had demonstrated their defiance of the original coroner's verdict, and left the clear message that they could call upon the extensive resources of the Chee Kong Tong and Chinese Six Companies when necessary."[105]

Meanwhile, according to the *Sentinel*, "The anti-Chinese agitation seems to be going forward like a prairie fire."[106] Hotels dismissed Chinese cooks and stewards, and some laundries went bankrupt. Despite the furor, leaders of the local Congregational church joined the denomination's statewide movement to "educate and Christianize" the Chinese. With unflinching support from Reverend William Pond, the leader of the church's outreach effort headquartered in San Francisco, they created a welcoming Chinese Mission. Located conveniently on Front Street, it was two doors down from Wong Kee's brick building. Not all Sunday school students became converts, but a significant number learned English, a major goal of the mission. In addition to the language lessons, "the Chinese came to the Christian missions for companionship, for legal protection and social mobility,"[107] according to Lydon. Moreover, to be culturally relevant, Congregationalists focused their teaching on Christian ethics, a topic consistent with the teachings of Confucius.

Wong Kee generously made several small loans to friends eager to leave Santa Cruz, but most of his $2,500 could not be returned, "as the Chinamen are unable to repay him on account of their non-employment by the white race."[108] In the midst of all this, Wong Kee's wife's health became paramount, but despite his all-out efforts, no cure could be found for her illness. "Mrs. Wong Kee, one of the very few women in Chinatown,

Columnist Ernest Otto fondly remembered the Chinese Mission on Front Street: "Written on the wall in Chinese characters were the Lord's Prayer and Ten Commandments." *Courtesy of MAH.*

was buried in Evergreen Cemetery Saturday afternoon with appropriate Chinese ceremonies. The bedding and clothes belonging to the deceased were burned at the grave. Roast pig, chickens and punks were placed on the grave by Wong Kee. After the mourners left the cemetery, a gang of tramps who had followed the funeral carried away the pig and chickens and had a feast."[109] Ernest Otto recalled many years later that after his wife's passing, Wong Kee had "a large photograph of her in his room and kept a light or taper burning continually before it."[110]

Despite reversals, Chinatown residents led by Wong Kee did their best to weather the storm of the "Chinese Must Go" movement. Several Santa Cruzans continued to buy from Chinese businesses, and three well-known pioneer families renewed their farmland leases with the entrepreneurial market gardeners.

The Freemasons seized an opportunity to register another protest at Evergreen in 1893. The occasion was motivated by a devastating blow: the United States Supreme Court's decision to uphold the ten-year extension of the Chinese Exclusion Act. With the death of one of their well-respected members, the brotherhood organized a ceremony consisting "of all the pomp and glory that Chinatown is capable of producing on funeral occasions." The orator enumerated the virtues of the deceased:

"He came to Santa Cruz twenty-four years ago a poor man, but by close attention to the vegetable business…he accumulated enough to engage in mercantile pursuits." Significantly, the concluding remark was one of objection to the court's ruling: "The deceased has gone to a place where he can't be deported."[111]

On the catastrophic night of April 14, 1894, Chinatown, the county courthouse and a block of businesses on Pacific Avenue went up in flames. All the Front Street buildings—the Chinese stores, apartments and other enterprises, including the Congregational Chinese Mission and the Chinese Freemason's Joss House—were annihilated. Because insurance companies had refused to cover his business, Wong Kee suffered heavy losses. But the community, although diminished, persevered with uncanny resilience. The spectacular 1896 Venetian Water Carnival, drawing well-wishers from San Jose, San Francisco and beyond, celebrated a rebuilt Santa Cruz, now with two Chinatown locations. Men from both areas played in a lively band atop their float, part of the festive parade down the San Lorenzo River.

Members of the reconstructed Congregational Chinese Mission are joined by Reverend William Pond of San Francisco, a regular visitor. To his right are teacher Mamie Perkins and Ah Yum, one of the few children in Chinatown. *Courtesy of MAH.*

A STAND FOR TRADITION

The anti-Chinese contingent felt victory within their reach by the turn of the century. The *Sentinel* provided its view: "The exclusion act and the steam laundry are too much for the Celestial. Those here die or go back to China. Those in the Orient are kept out of this country. Their extinction in California, unless the law of exclusion is changed, is inevitable."[112]

During this very dark hour, Wong Kee embraced the priority of the remaining Chinese: to ensure their dead would be handled properly regardless of what lay ahead politically. The *Surf* reported, "The Chinese who have died and been buried in this city have always been interred in a plot on the side hill adjoining the potters' field. A movement is now on foot among the local Chinese to buy a plot in the Evergreen cemetery, have it fenced and to be used entirely by them as a burying ground."[113]

Wong Kee led the Freemasons' prolonged negotiations with the Evergreen Cemetery Association and the county. Evidently, a deposit of $300, contributed mostly by Chinatown merchants, secured the Chinese area and set off a celebration with a record number of firecrackers. This detailed description ran in the *Surf*:

> *There is a slab upon which to place the offerings and in which are a number of holes where the punk and candles, which are always burned at a funeral, can be placed. Back of the altar and at the sides is a low wall and placed in the wall is a marble tablet on which is engraved in English, "Chinese Burial Ground, February 1, 1901."*[114]

LOCAL SUPPORT

As a denomination, the local Congregationalists were alone in their outreach. In fact, Elihu Anthony, a founder of the Methodist church, became one of the most vitriolic voices for the anti-Chinese and pro-labor contingent. His rhetoric, anathema to Methodist teachings, led three members of the author's family to a heart-wrenching decision. The Blisses, although multigenerational Methodists, felt they had no choice but to resign from the church. They became Congregationalists in the 1890s, where they could actively support the Chinese Mission.

Members of the Congregational church eagerly showcased the mission's accomplishments to the entire community. Lem Sam, at age nineteen, became one of the Sunday school's first pupils and participated in recitals for a standing-room-only crowd in 1884. He first sang the solo section of a hymn, then shared with the audience "his trials and tribulations" learning English. Concluding the program, Reverend Mahlon Willett proudly introduced Lem Sam and four others as the newest church members. When he became sufficiently proficient in spoken and written English, Lem Sam worked as an interpreter for the superior court, but with a dwindling Chinese population, demand fell off. He then supported himself serving as a cook for local families.

Lem Sam, also a member of the Freemasons, shared a strong sense of community with others in the radical group, committed to traditional Chinese values. For him, in contrast to most Chinatown residents, membership in both organizations made sense. When the Congregational mission reopened on Bellevue Place, after the 1894 fire, he began performing once again at annual public recitals. A special celebration of the mission's twentieth anniversary in 1901 featured Lem Sam's rendition of "I Am a Pilgrim" to the appreciative crowd. Restored to church membership after a temporary lapse, he gratefully accepted an upstairs room at the mission.

Lem Sam (*at center with open book*) leads his fellow students at the Chinese Mission. *Special Collections, University Library, University of California–Santa Cruz. Santa Cruz County Historic Photograph Collection.*

On the lookout for more work, Lem Sam and his friend Ah Fong went job-hunting in the Seabright neighborhood. The men took a shortcut home by walking across the railroad bridge at the mouth of the San Lorenzo River. When a freight train barreled toward them around a blind curve, Ah Fong jumped down to the sand, but Lem Sam suffered fatal injuries. United in grief, his community honored their friend with a unique funeral that combined his two cultures. The Freemasons led the procession, followed by most of the local Chinese. Then, at the cemetery itself, a Congregational minister conducted a Christian burial service for Lem Sam, probably the first of its kind in the Chinese section of Evergreen.

The horrific death mobilized the tightknit community of Seabright in a concerted fundraising effort followed by negotiations with the railroad. They succeeded in installing a permanent footbridge on the dangerous trestle in 1905. After more than a century of use, hundreds of locals celebrated the footbridge's stunning renovation. The expanded walkway/trail opened in time for the summer onslaught in 2019.

THE END OF AN ERA

Wong Kee's leadership and reverence for tradition reminded Chinese expatriates of their common roots. Early in the new century, Wong Kee yielded his unofficial title to Woo Gap, a newcomer who would preside over a fast-diminishing community. In 1912, with the overthrow of the imperial government in China, the requirement for men to have a queue hairstyle ended. What could be more symbolic than Wong Kee's visit to the barber? A reporter for the *Surf* remarked, "One of the best known of the old time Chinese is one of the last to part with his queue....As a Freemason and past master of the Chee Kong Tong, he has been an ardent revolutionist, and with the rest he finally allowed his queue to be taken off and now he is very proud of what he has done."[115] Wong Kee's passing in November 1926 inspired an uncommon tribute—an editorial in the *Sentinel*:

> *Wong Kee was a good citizen because he was a good man. He was a builder and yet Fate did not treat him kindly and fire destroyed his buildings, but he smiled and carried on. Kee did not stop to cry over his losses....He lived in Santa Cruz for over fifty years. Wong Kee was a past master of the Chinese Freemasons. Yes, he was a good citizen of the land of his adoption.*[116]

With many of his Chinatown friends already interred at their Evergreen burial ground, only a handful were left to attend his quiet funeral. But his American friends filled several cars, making a long procession behind the hearse. They gathered to say farewell at the site Wong Kee had masterfully secured a quarter of a century earlier. "A brick with his name upon it was placed in the ground, so that when the bones are dug up to be sent to China they could be identified."[117]

A decade later, Wong Kee's bones, along with those of six other local residents, were picked up for transportation home. But they never left the West Coast due to the Japanese invasion of China seven months later in 1937. Their ultimate destination remains a mystery.[118]

Chapter 10

A FAMILY LEGACY

THE SEXTON

In 1880s Santa Cruz, <u>Seth Blanchard</u> shared a brief written biography with his fellow members of the local Society of California Pioneers. The adventurer did not mention that he'd been a Methodist minister in Massachusetts or that he had left behind his wife, Lucy Shepard Blanchard, and their daughter when he headed to California in 1849. He did, however, note his various locations searching for treasure in the gold fields.[119]

An unexpected connection with <u>Johan Carl Labish</u> in Calaveras County provided Blanchard with a new opportunity outside the mines. His Saxony-born friend, a skilled blacksmith and noted swordsman, had crossed the plains in the 1840s with his wife, <u>Augusta</u>, and infant daughter, <u>Albertina</u>. Though Labish settled in Branciforte, he later also owned a ranch on the Calaveras River where he hired the well-educated Blanchard to tutor Albertina and his five young sons in 1856.

After a few years with the Labish family, the tenacious Blanchard resumed working various claims, often alongside Chinese miners. Although he never struck gold in a big way, he did master the art of using a pick and shovel for moving earth. Finally calling it quits at age forty-three, he visited his Santa Cruz friends, having never forgotten his former pupil. Just two weeks after Seth reconnected with twenty-three-year-old Albertina Labish, the pair exchanged vows at the Congregational church. Two years later in 1867, she

Originally a minister in New England and then a gold miner, Seth Blanchard became a consistent presence at Evergreen. Beginning in the 1870s, he served as the cemetery's first sexton. *Tefertiller family collection.*

gave birth to twin boys, <u>Seth Jr.</u> and <u>Albert</u>, followed by three daughters. Their prolific marriage managed to survive the shock of his first wife's showing up. Lucy had moved to San Francisco in 1870, apparently with unrealistic hopes for reconciliation.

Evergreen Cemetery trustees quickly realized that Blanchard's skills with a shovel suited their needs and appointed him the first official sexton, responsible for grave digging and plot maintenance. With excavation expertise that extended well beyond the cemetery boundary, he also worked as a local contractor. One Blanchard project consisted of making the tracks between the San Lorenzo River and Seabright Station for F.A. Hihn's railroad. Seth probably took the most pride in creating the foundation for the new school on Mission Hill that his and Albertina's children attended. As for his daughter and son by Lucy, his first wife, they showed up in Santa Cruz in 1882. Was this visit with Seth[120] the siblings' first contact with their sixty-year-old father? Perhaps they learned that his diverse set of talents included a gift for languages: he spoke English, French, Spanish and German and served as a translator.[121]

STONECUTTERS

Perhaps there was never a more ideal decade at Evergreen than the 1890s. A robust cadre of supporters helped maintain the Victorian ambience, and the cemetery averaged at least a few dozen burials a year. Moreover, the artistic quality of the monuments improved dramatically with the arrival of John Henry Bilodeau in the late 1880s, after practicing the stone carver's trade for a decade in his native New England. The redheaded newcomer, a descendant of French stonemasons, operated on an unprecedented scale, importing whole freight cars of marble and granite. When his work at Evergreen brought him into contact with sexton Blanchard, romance followed soon after. John married Seth and Albertina's daughter, Laura, in January 1889. Unfortunately, just eleven months later, one of Bilodeau's monuments would be for his father-in-law, who died of heart failure. Seth Blanchard's many friends at the Pioneer Society conducted an elaborate burial ritual at Evergreen.

Bilodeau's Santa Cruz Marble and Granite Works prospered, with all the local cemeteries featuring his tombstones. He kept detailed diaries of customers' requests, which included the Chinese community. Preferring granite to marble and with an unrelenting commitment to first-class material, he selected every stone himself. At his quarry near Scotts Valley's Granite Creek, he delighted in discovering an entire ledge of stunning sky-blue stone.

For a time after the 1894 fire, there were two Chinatowns in Santa Cruz, but decreased population caused a consolidation in 1905. Bilodeau partnered with the proprietor of the surviving downtown neighborhood, supervising the moving and reconstruction of dwellings. Edna Bilodeau liked to tell the story of going with her father in the buggy on trips down to Chinatown. She said the Chinese would come out and give her little gifts, including ornate boxes, one of which still remains in the family.

Widely known for his integrity, Bilodeau crafted most of the headstones and vaults throughout Santa Cruz County. After thirty-two years in business, he died suddenly of diabetes in 1919. Masons poured into Wessendorf and Sons funeral home, offering their farewell to a member who'd held almost every role in the local lodge. Grace Delamater Williamson sang at the service and most likely selected a John Wesley hymn to honor John Henry Bilodeau's decades of membership in the Methodist church.

When Santa Cruzans lost their revered stone carver, there was no one locally to take over the business. Laura, John's wife, turned to her daughter Edna and cowboy son-in-law Orie Dunlap, living in Greenfield. The young

John Henry Bilodeau and his wife, Laura, daughter of Seth Blanchard, pose with their daughters, Edna (*standing*) and Grace (*on John's lap*), in 1898. *Tefertiller family collection.*

Above: Residents throughout the region relied on the Santa Cruz Marble and Granite Works. When John Bilodeau died suddenly, his son-in-law quickly learned the business. *Tefertiller family collection.*

Left: After working as a cowboy in his youth, Orie Dunlap owned and operated the Marble and Granite Works while pursuing a career in law enforcement. He battled corruption relentlessly in the 1930s. *Tefertiller family collection.*

Although Santa Cruz Granite and Marble closed in the 1960s, John Bilodeau's mallet for gravestone carving is well preserved. His quality stones included many selected from quarries in Vermont. *Tefertiller family collection.*

couple returned to Santa Cruz, and Orie, an accomplished carpenter, learned a new trade. With no prior experience in stonecutting, he continued the family tradition of fine craftsmanship throughout the Roaring Twenties.

While still directing the Marble and Granite Works, Dunlap took on a major responsibility near the end of Prohibition. Santa Cruz became enmeshed in a corruption scandal that sent Chief of Police William Walker to San Quentin for accepting bribes from bootleggers. Dunlap took over as chief in August 1932 and restored integrity to the tarnished department. He cleared up eighty-five burglaries and made forty-nine arrests for liquor and gambling before a stunning event in April 1933, when a shakeup on the city council led to his firing. The councilman making the decision had twice gone to trial for accepting bribes from bootleggers.

After that, Dunlap spent most of the rest of the 1930s serving as chief criminal deputy for the Sheriff's Department, investigating major crimes in the county. In 1952, for his brother Clyde's gravestone, Dunlap used one of his own designs—the "Jesus with a lamb" image—very much in demand locally. He lived until 1966 and was interred at Evergreen, followed by his wife, Edna, four years later. Santa Cruz Marble and Granite closed upon Dunlap's death. His son-in-law, Earl Tefertiller, and Earl's son, Casey Orie Tefertiller, crafted Orie's headstone. Fittingly, it bore a prominent sheriff's badge and was the final marker to come from the business.

ADVOCATES

Albertina Blanchard, Seth's Santa Cruz wife, lived to be ninety-two. Upon her death in 1934, she was interred in the family plot at Evergreen, and her eldest daughter, Laura Blanchard Bilodeau, would be buried nearby ten years later. Meanwhile, Albertina's youngest daughter and namesake, Albertina Blanchard Westfall, had left Santa Cruz early on to pursue her career as a graphic artist in San Francisco. Returning home in the 1950s, she regularly visited the family plot, determined to improve the cemetery's down-at-the-heels appearance. A vigilant volunteer, Albertina organized rummage sales to benefit the Evergreen Association. Her passing in 1958 inspired a *Sentinel* editorial:

> *To her, Evergreen Cemetery was far more than a graveyard, it was a place of historic interest, a tranquil and beautiful spot, deserving of the everlasting consideration of the community. It would be especially fitting if renewed interest in the improvement of the Evergreen Cemetery could be forthcoming this year.*[122]

In 2004, Ruby Dunlap Tefertiller, Orie and Edna's daughter, joined her ancestors at Evergreen. During World War II, she became one of the first two women to serve in the Santa Cruz Police Department. Her several local causes included many years of membership in the Santa Cruz Historical Society, which consistently advocated for Evergreen. Ruby was the fifth generation to be buried at the cemetery: Labish, Blanchard, Bilodeau, Dunlap and Tefertiller. In dedicating a book to his mother, Casey Tefertiller captured the essence of a multigenerational legacy: Ruby's unflinching belief that miracles can happen with enough hard work.

Chapter 11

WHAT WOULD THE TWENTIETH CENTURY BRING?

In the Victorian era, cemeteries throughout America symbolized deep-seated values about community and duty to one's fellow man; they were a tangible display of how the living showed their obligation to the dead. Evergreen embodied Emerson's ideal of "nature as a language"—a garden-like sanctuary away from the beaten path where one found harmony and repose. One newcomer to Santa Cruz, <u>DeEtte Newcomb</u>, "discovered" the uniquely nestled beauty in the early 1900s. With no relatives buried at Evergreen, she loved the charming wooded glen for its own sake. That discovery would begin a family commitment that deepened in the 1920s and continues today.

THE GREAT WAR

With World War I raging, thousands of Santa Cruz County's men registered for the draft, a requirement of the U.S. Selective Service Act in May 1917. Close to 3,500 locals enlisted, and by the end of the conflict, 60 had died. Only one of those—<u>Grayson Lacy Wilkerson</u>, son of the First Christian Church pastor—can be found at Evergreen. When still a toddler, Grayson had moved with his family from Pomona, California, to Vine Hill, and at age nineteen he enlisted, assigned to the Cavalry Branch at Fort McDowell on Angel Island. The fort lacked appropriate housing, and despite excessive illness among the soldiers, medical personnel were in short supply. Just a month after pledging to serve his country, Grayson contracted pneumonia and died.

THE 1920s AND THE GREAT DEPRESSION

By 1921, nearly 70 percent of what ultimately would be the total number of burials had occurred. The two remaining association trustees, Frank Heath and Della Perry, had just passed on, and Della's husband, Charles—intent on preserving pioneer heritage—took charge. An astute businessman, he made the Evergreen Cemetery Association official with articles of incorporation in 1922 and garnered thirty-three subscriptions at $1,000 each. A newly elected board of directors, all plot holders, included prominent names from early families such as Frank Cooper, Lillian Heath and Landreth Errington. One new trustee, Uriah M. Thompson, had a cherished legacy to protect as the great-grandson of Hiram and Ruth Imus and grandson of Judge Henry and Lucy Imus Rice. Profoundly concerned about the condition of Evergreen, Perry led the board in a strategic effort that included a controlled burn of the heavy underbrush, determined to "clean up and beautify this neglected spot."[123]

DeEtte Newcomb and her husband, Worthy, undertook another initiative creating an inviting iron-arched entrance gate. As a young couple living in Nebraska in the 1880s, they had lost their eight-year-old daughter, Glen Gertrude, and one-and-a-half-year-old son, Wayne, to scarlet fever, both on the same day. The gate honored these two siblings. With this type of renewed activity, did the cemetery now have a more solid footing? Worthy Newcomb intended to make that happen. Having wound down his management of the Newcomb family fruit farm on Granite Creek Road, he joined the Evergreen Association Board of Trustees.

But Worthy had too little time to make an impact, dying suddenly in 1924. DeEtte now fully embraced the burial ground as her calling. Not surprisingly, the petite grandmother's activism had deep roots. She had grown up in Ohio, reared on the stories of her father's and grandfather's involvement in the Underground Railroad. Later, as a well-educated teacher, she publicly spoke out for women's rights. A prolific writer, she used her way with words to draw attention to the cemetery. She penned the first in a series of letters

Charles Perry stands on the steps of the Perry House, which his father, John Perry, designed and built in 1853. The current owners are committed to preserving this historic landmark on Escalona Drive. *Judith Steen Collection.*

to the *Santa Cruz News* in 1925, making the case for putting Evergreen on "a business basis," and promoted the availability of many more plots than the public believed existed. Thanks to her efforts, regular maintenance and beautification were supported by an endowment. DeEtte proudly told Santa Cruzans, "That which was fast becoming a reproach shall become instead an object of civic pride."[124]

DeEtte eagerly planted roses, shrubs and trees to restore the erstwhile tranquil beauty. Meanwhile, the city installed a new water system, made possible through private donations. The Newcombs' dedication redefined Evergreen advocacy; responsibility for preserving the precious place no longer rested primarily with descendants of the original plot holders.

Both DeEtte Newcomb and Charles Perry, who had diligently carried on the dedication of their respective spouses, died in the early 1930s. Who would step in now as challenges mounted? In the preceding decade, Evergreen had averaged fifteen burials per year; now the annual count was around eight. During the Depression, grieving families were far less

EVERGREEN CEMETERY

RATES

Price of Lots 20x20 feet; including perpetual care:

Full Lot	$350.00
½ Lot, 20x10	225.00
¼ Lot, 10x10	150.00
Single Graves	75.00

PERPETUAL CARE

Full Lot	$250.00
½ Lot	150.00
¼ Lot	100·00
Single Grave	50.00

YEARLY CARE

Full Lot	$10.00
½ Lot	6.00
¼ Lot	4.00
Single Grave	3.00
Digging Grave	10.00

Board of Directors by

WORTHY T. NEWCOMB,
Supt. of Grounds.

Above: In the 1920s, volunteers DeEtte Newcomb and her son Leighton look out from the Glory Path to the surrounding overgrowth. *Newcomb family collection.*

Left: Courtesy of MAH.

likely to invest in headstones, donations for maintenance fell way off and competition proliferated. The nearby IOOF Cemetery, for example, offered what Evergreen could not: huge plots, easy access to all burial locations and intact records.

GRIEF BECOMES COMMITMENT

For <u>Charles</u> and <u>LaSalle Bachelder</u>, Evergreen provided a path forward from tragedy. Charles grew up on the Granite Creek Road family ranch, where he developed his cattle ranching skills and became a member of the Episcopal church and Masonic Lodge, while his wife, LaSalle, taught in the one-room Happy Valley schoolhouse. She was a no-nonsense teacher. If her students fought during recess, LaSalle required them to "get it out of their systems at lunch time" by slapping trees with fallen branches.[125]

The couple's only child, <u>Celeste</u>, excelled at Santa Cruz High School and planned to graduate in June 1936. But the celebration never happened; in late May, she fell from her horse and days later died from a fractured skull. Charles and LaSalle buried her next to <u>John Arthur</u>, Charles's brother, who had died a few weeks after his birth. For the next forty years, the couple stayed close by: Charles assumed the role of Evergreen Association president, and LaSalle took on all correspondence as secretary.

The Bachelders worked with Uriah M. Thompson, a descendant of the Imus/ Rice clan, to improve the cemetery's shaky finances. Thompson informed the press that the association's annual income— eighty dollars in interest from government bonds—was hardly adequate to maintain the grounds. After an unsuccessful fund drive, the cemetery directors decided to purchase an adjacent acre of land. Although some neighbors objected to the extension, the Bachelders and Thompson convinced the city council to issue the necessary permits and, in 1942, offered new plots for sale.

Soon after she posed for her graduation picture, Celeste Sylvia Bachelder's untimely death stunned her classmates. Six of her girlfriends from Santa Cruz High served as honorary pallbearers. *Courtesy of SCHS Alumni Association.*

Standing at the Blackburn family plot, the Bachelders inspect the depleted Cloud family plot with a broken marker on the ground. *Courtesy of MAH.*

WORLD WAR II

Nearly 6,000 Santa Cruz County residents and former residents registered for the draft within a month of the Selective Service Act's passage in September 1940. Of the 245 who made the ultimate sacrifice, around four dozen were laid to rest in county cemeteries. Only Evergreen did not attract a single memorial. Ninety years earlier, locals had solemnly gathered for the cemetery's first public burial. Was it now just a lonesome artifact of an erstwhile era?

For one native Santa Cruzan, the early pioneers' stories would be remembered in a fresh way for a dedicated weekly audience. Sociable Clifford Neil Kilfoyl, a professional printer, became one of the earliest members of

Riding on Pacific Avenue, Clifford Kilfoyl enjoys his role as grand marshal of the Santa Cruz Fiesta parade in October 1946. *Courtesy of Nancy Kilfoyl Campeau.*

Santa Cruz Rotary and quite enjoyed Saturday nights at the Boardwalk's Casino Ballroom. On one such evening, Grace DeLamater Williamson, the Casino's official chaperone, connected Cliff with her daughter <u>Edith</u>. Marriage soon followed, and the couple moved in with Grace; the Ocean View estate proved ideal for her son-in-law. A passionate rodeo rider, he transformed Grace's backyard for his horses and a riding ring.

A decade later, while serving as president of the chamber of commerce, Cliff expanded his Santa Cruz Printery, where he and Edith could work in tandem. Publishing the weekly *Riptide* newspaper, they relished promoting Santa Cruz history through rare photos of yesteryear and in-depth articles on early pioneers. When the family moved to the sprawling, rural dairy farms of Scotts Valley, the area was well suited to Cliff's "don't fence me in" cowboy persona. Although the *Riptide* stopped publishing in 1953, he managed the printing business for another decade, ushering in a new era of lithography. With dramatic color printing, he took special pride in brochures such as one for Brown's Bulb Ranch featuring a dazzling array of begonias. As for Kilfoyl's legacy, local historians treasure the *Riptide* archives, located at the Museum of Art and History. These artifacts, especially the illustrations, offer a unique window into the pioneer era.

Cliff's mother-in-law, Grace, whose life is detailed in chapter 8, established the precedent for supporting Evergreen. While a working widow, she still managed to generously contribute to the cemetery's maintenance. In contrast to progeny of some other pioneer families who had either succumbed at an early age or had moved out of the area, DeLamater descendants carried on with a wholehearted commitment to the burial ground during its most challenging times.

EVERGREEN'S SECOND CENTURY

The postwar baby boom ensured that Santa Cruz prospered, but that did not include the unremembered inhabitants of Evergreen. Burials averaged five per year, and the cumulative effect of deferred maintenance seemed unconquerable for the dwindling group of volunteers. Some who attended Santa Cruz High School in the '50s recall a haunted place reminiscent of Edgar Allan Poe's ghoulish writings. Broken headstones, abandoned plots and the invasive, tangled myrtle vines created a darkly mysterious and spooky place. Eerie Evergreen had become a magnet for underage drinking and bad behavior.

Wally Trabing, a prominent local columnist for the *Sentinel*, expressed outrage over community neglect: "At present it is a disgrace and eyesore to the city. Because of its appearance of abandonment, it breeds the thrill-seeking interest of vandals. The people who were laid to rest here bequeathed their heritage to this city, and their memories deserve a better fate."[126] Trabing had the right exhortation at the wrong time. In 1958 and continuing for five years, local energy galvanized around a campaign to attract a University of California campus. Ebullient politicians, business leaders and service clubs pulled out all stops to promote the majestic natural beauty of the proposed UCSC campus.[127] Meanwhile, a mere mile away, the Victorian garden that had once been Evergreen lay mostly in ruins.

Nonetheless, the Bachelders managed to capitalize on the increased state and national interest in historic preservation. In 1968, with support from the Daughters of the American Revolution, the Native Sons of the Golden West

Cemetery caretakers struggled to overcome mischief caused by vandals, who knocked A.A. Taylor's memorial off its pedestal and frequently stole markers. *Courtesy of MAH.*

and the Santa Cruz County Historical Society, they achieved recognition for the cemetery as a Point of Historical Interest for the State of California. But resources for even basic maintenance remained elusive.

TWENTY YEARS OF REVIVAL

Charles and LaSalle always welcomed friends and strangers to their historic Granite Creek ranch and did likewise at Evergreen, despite its deplorable condition. When Charles passed on in 1973 at age eighty-seven, how prescient his parting thoughts: "Someday people who care about those who made this town what it is will help us get the paths to look like paths again. We have wanted that so long."[128]

LaSalle successfully implored Margaret Koch, a history columnist for the *Santa Cruz Sentinel*, to become the Evergreen Association president. Koch eagerly produced a two-page article titled "Do You Care?" in July 1973. She focused on community involvement and Evergreen's charismatic new champion, Renie Leaman, who called herself a "cemetery nut."

When folks from throughout the county converged to help with Leaman's massive cleanup, Sandy Lydon brought his Asian American history class from Cabrillo College to join the labor force. He recalled, "Though the day was hotter than hell, the students really dug in."[129] The class even found a carved brick from a Chinese grave, a tradition consistently used for identification. Lydon continued to stay in contact with Renie to help with her herculean effort.

Lydon's work at Evergreen added to his research on the largely forgotten history of Santa Cruz's Chinese community, brought to life in his now-classic *Chinese Gold: The Chinese in the Monterey Bay Region*. He offers this summary of the Chinese experience at Evergreen:

> *Cemeteries often provide the best uncensored history of a place. Despite the truism that the grave silences all temporal matters, the dead do tell tales. The true history lies beyond the words carved into the tombstones; it's in the geography. Evergreen Cemetery is a horizontal blueprint of Santa Cruz's history.*
>
> *The crowd's chant of "The Chinese Must Go" is echoed in the location of the Chinese section. Ostracized and vilified in life, the Chinese were consigned to a distant corner of the cemetery. Racist laws mandated that they would forever be aliens, and they died alone in this hostile landscape. Then their bones were exhumed and shipped to China so they could spend their eternities in the comfort of their family. Most of the graves in the Chinese section are empty. And over the decades their stories and contributions were lost, obscured by weeds and neglect.*
>
> *Then in the 1970s the histories began to change. Inspired by a renewed interest in hearing the many unknown stories that Evergreen could tell, Santa Cruz expanded its historical vision and became determined to give the Chinese the honor and respect they never received in life.*[130]

By incorporating the nonprofit HELP (Help Evergreen Live Permanently), Leaman consolidated a variety of resources for ongoing

Professor Sandy Lydon and his Asian American history class from Cabrillo College dig in during the massive Evergreen cleanup organized by HELP (Help Evergreen Live Permanently). *Photo by Bill Lovejoy.*

Promoting local history, Renie Leaman and Professor Sandy Lydon discuss some of her Evergreen materials at a Branciforte library event in 1977. *Photo by Bill Lovejoy.*

maintenance: service group volunteers, individuals hired through the Comprehensive Employment Training Act (CETA), army reserves and court referrals. Concurrently, she designed the first uniform system for collecting data on the interred. Once both initiatives were well underway, Renie could pursue her primary passion of researching dramatic stories to engage folks in the cultural heritage embodied by the interred. Visitors to Evergreen had a choice of topics: blacks, children, pioneers, politicians and women—all brought to life with the aid of her stunning collection of historic hats.

Having led more than 250 tours by 1985, Renie now had the help of a full-time volunteer with a passion for local history. Joan Nelson had no expertise with archives but with great determination set out to restore hundreds of lost files. "She persisted in reaching out to families because there was no one else to do it," reported her husband, Robert Nelson. "Renie and Joan supported

Above, left: The Loma Prieta earthquake of 1989 shattered the Imus obelisk commemorating the burial grounds' originators. *Courtesy of MAH.*

Above, right: Francis and Almira Kittredges' two children died during the Civil War period. The family's monument turned forty-five degrees during the earthquake. *Courtesy of MAH.*

Opposite: A renowned stone conservator from Mexico City, Alejandro Reyes-Vizzuett leads the massive restoration effort at Evergreen. *Courtesy of MAH.*

each other through thick and thin, giving more than their all because there were never enough Evergreen volunteers."

By 1986, Leaman had found a much-needed sponsor. The Santa Cruz County Historical Trust was created through a merger of the Santa Cruz Historical Society and the Octagon Historical Trust. With an unrelenting Renie serving on the board, the new organization assumed responsibility for Evergreen, giving it an organizational home for the first time. The trust was a major force behind the growing momentum for historic preservation countywide. President Cynthia Mathews produced a thorough and engaging monthly newsletter, ensuring that Evergreen finally had found its niche as part of a dynamic movement. Mathews and Lehman together created the cover story for the May 1988 edition: "Rediscovering Evergreen Cemetery." The piece promoted a new Evergreen brochure and celebrated more than a decade of "organized effort to rescue the cemetery from years of near neglect."[131]

Devastating as it was, the Loma Prieta earthquake of 1989 brought about a once-in-a-lifetime opportunity. With FEMA funds supplemented by local donations, Evergreen showcased high-quality cemetery restoration. Alejandro Reyes, a conservation specialist trained in Mexico City, led a crew in stabilizing and preserving thirty-four gravestones that had been toppled or damaged by the quake. "He brought such expertise and commitment to the sustainability of the monuments," says Rachel McKay, who served as collection manager for the Trust.

REMEMBERING A WELL-KNOWN FELLOW

Inspired by Alejandro's work, Mary Wood, a retired Dominican Hospital administrator and Renie's dedicated protégé for historic tours, felt something had to be done to restore the vandalized grave of London Nelson. Wood reached out to her friend and co-worker at Dominican, Francile Hill, who gladly connected Mary with friends at the NAACP. Her pitch to the organization had a surprise ending: in 1993, the City of Santa Cruz stepped in with funds to restore London Nelson's grave, while the NAACP supported the restoration of George Andrew Chester's gravestone.

Since Chester had not previously been part of Evergreen history tours, the NAACP's interest prompted research into his many decades as a well-known local. Born in Philadelphia in 1830 as a free man, George

As a regular docent, Mary Wood led dozens of history tours that always included stories of the Arcan family, Isaac Graham and London Nelson. *Courtesy of MAH.*

Andrew Chester arrived in Santa Cruz with his wife and three children in the 1860s. Soon after, his wife passed on, leaving George a single parent. This would be the first of innumerable challenges he met with optimism and flexibility.

After marrying his second wife, Mary Theresa, he became an entrepreneur in the food business. His unique ice cream recipe earned him a reputation for making special events special, like the Fourth of July at Bausch's Beer Garden. When he opened a downtown restaurant offering coffee, biscuits, steaks and stews, he promised "a meal with toothsome relish and some nice wine or ale to wash it down."[132]

In spite of some setbacks, George kept at it, advertising his latest venture—the Saddle Rock Oyster Saloon—in May 1875. Sadly, however, the same issue of the *Sentinel* contained the death notice for Mary Theresa at age twenty-five. By the next tourist season, George could be found at the beach serving oysters and coffee at the Liddell Bath House. Meanwhile, he married a widow from Watsonville, adopted her son and enjoyed a union that lasted for the rest of his life. As local historian Phil

Posters advertising a show by the famous heavyweight champion John L. Sullivan decorate the front of the Santa Cruz Opera House in 1891. The venue continued to attract touring companies until the 1920s. *Courtesy of MAH.*

San Lorenzo Valley artisan Cliff Short carved the replacement marker for George Chester's grave in 1993, but a tree crushed it a few years later. The marker was restored a second time in 2016. *Courtesy of MAH.*

Reader observed, "Chester also became a kind of spokesman for blacks who moved to or just visited Santa Cruz. Often he and his family would put them up at his house and he went out of his way to make sure they had jobs."[133]

Although he left the risky restaurant business, Chester's culinary reputation opened doors. When F.A. Hihn hosted his grand Society of California Pioneers picnic, Chester supervised the coffee service for hundreds of guests. Eventually, he found steady income as a janitor for the Santa Cruz Opera House, and what an opportunity! George saw his grown daughter in two performances in the early 1880s. Miss Georgie Chester, a featured cornet player, belonged to one of the few nonwhite traveling minstrel shows, and the *Sentinel* gave special mention to Georgie, "who blew a brass horn and sang on the stage."[134]

By the end of the century, Chester had reinvented himself again with a successful shoe-shine business on Pacific Avenue. His *Sentinel* advertisement showed his usual flair for words: "To the Ladies! You may have your shoes neatly polished, any color, in front of W.P. Carr's shoe shop, the neatest place in town—inside and out of the heat or cold. George A. Chester"[135]

When he passed on at age seventy-six, George Andrew Chester's obituary observed that "he was known to practically everybody."[136]

ELUSIVE SUSTAINABILITY

Throughout the 1990s, the fun of performing mini-portrayals of individuals interred at Evergreen had taken on a life of its own. Santa Cruzans had long enjoyed a penchant for costumed drama, and the cemetery provided a picturesque outdoor venue.

But public awareness of Evergreen's needs and accomplishments—successfully achieved by the Santa Cruz County Historical Trust over several years—had begun to wane. Two volunteers, pillars of Leaman's efforts, had moved on: Cynthia Mathews to the city council and Mary Wood to Arizona. Moreover, Evergreen had new ownership because several organizations had merged to create the Museum of Art and History in 1996. With the exhilaration of a beautiful new building made possible by the McPherson family, coupled with leadership eager to promote art, Evergreen began to slip back into obscurity and neglect.

Some well-known figures from Evergreen's past are included in this 1997 reenactment by local performers. *Left to right*: Peter McGettigan, Dee Kraft, Kathryn Kinsar, Katie LeBaron and Jeff Caplan as Henry Thompson, Renie Leaman as Eliza Boston, Dart Keech as Isaac Graham and Pat Clark as London Nelson. *Courtesy of MAH.*

Live Oak Elementary teacher Shelby Henderson engages her audience, including local historian and writer Joan Martin in the wide-brimmed hat. Joan's daughter, Rachel McKay, wears a flowered bonnet. *Courtesy of MAH.*

For the next decade and beyond, the Evergreen Committee, down to a handful of volunteers, soldiered on with tours, gravestone cleaning and whatever help it could manage to round up. So, too, the Branciforte chapter of E Clampus Vitus (the Clampers) continued with clearing paths and restoring fences—a commitment they have honored for over a quarter of a century. Both groups never considered giving up, despite mounting challenges.

Chapter 12

EVERGREEN'S
RENAISSANCE

WHAT CAN BE DONE?

As I wandered among the earliest graves at Evergreen at the beginning of 2009, the forlorn headstones haunted me. Once-upright pillars of the past now rested full length on the ground, broken if not forgotten relics, including those of my fourth great-grandparents, Hiram and Ruth Imus. Was the unselfish community spirit that had repeatedly revived this sacred space now broken beyond repair? What, if anything, could I contribute?

The answer soon came when I accepted the invitation to join the Museum of Art and History Board of Trustees. Having recently retired early from my career as an education professor, I wanted to contribute to the community where I grew up. Prior to my first board meeting, executive director Paul Figueroa implored me to become the liaison to the Evergreen Committee, explaining up front that no other trustee would agree to the role. With the zeal of a convert (as explained in the prologue), I jumped at the opportunity, unaware that the scores of broken headstones only hinted at Evergreen's predicament.

In March, I began attending monthly meetings of the Evergreen Committee, a group that seemed dispirited and divided, despite the staff's upbeat minutes. Tensions ran high over the recently released *Evergreen Cemetery Preservation Plan* (February 6, 2009). The thorough review, called for in the *MAH Strategic Plan 2003–2008*, was more than a wake-up call. Edited by Judith Steen, a preservationist, historian and former UCSC librarian, the document revealed a dire situation put in historical context with convincing evidence and clarity. Many challenges are detailed in the document, such as the need for a modern data management system. However, one item was by far the most troubling for its perniciousness and corrosive impact. Significant erosion coupled with no systematic maintenance creates jungle-like overgrowth, leading to a host of other problems. The Preservation Plan addresses many consequences of neglect, including "drug use, occupation after hours and the dumping of garbage and human waste must be curtailed as these are extremely disrespectful to the families of those buried here."[137]

For a century, committed volunteer leaders had stepped in at key junctures to address chronic issues but never with adequate resources to permanently fix problems or to sustain momentum for notable gains. Now this comprehensive Preservation Plan, representing the work of a twelve-person committee of experts, community representatives and museum staff, provided a feasible path forward. But at least half the Evergreen Committee members at that time considered the plan's recommendations impossible to achieve. Essential resources had never been available, and the economic downturn coupled with MAH's financial troubles had pushed the cemetery even lower on the list of board priorities. Figueroa, though deeply committed to Evergreen and the history it embodied, had his hands full dealing with destructive camping on and around headstones and heavy rains inundating the Chinese section and Potters' Field.

What did other MAH trustees think of the Preservation Plan? Figueroa's best efforts to get it on the agenda never materialized. Some board members had always considered Evergreen an albatross that should have been the city's responsibility. I suggested we hold our July board meeting at the cemetery, and Figueroa embraced the idea. Several of the "first time at Evergreen" trustees were pleasantly surprised by the bucolic serenity and kempt appearance (thanks to the Memorial Day cleanup weeks earlier). Docents Joan Nelson and Georgie Lane, in period costumes, championed the importance of school tours for teaching fourth-graders local history, and I shared my family story of how Evergreen came to be. Having captured the board's attention, the time seemed ripe for me to plant a seed: "School tours have been a hallmark of Evergreen for decades. Let's make this a thriving outdoor experience for everyone."

Weeks later, Evergreen Committee chair Joan Nelson, bereft over deferred maintenance in the extreme, connected with an adventurous father at the cemetery. Gary Neier enjoyed exploring the nooks and crannies of Evergreen with his four-year-old son, Terry, and responded to Joan's request for help. His work initially focused on just trash removal and a weekly walk-through. However, encountering a number of "bad actors" living above the cemetery, it became clear that "Evergreen was not a welcoming place" and on the road to disaster. Changing the entire trajectory would require a massive effort.

A TURNING POINT: 2010–2011

With the Evergreen Committee's whole-hearted encouragement, Gary reached out to the newly formed "Take Back Santa Cruz" community group. At least 120 volunteers, including the Clampers, rolled up their sleeves to clean the pioneer cemetery. The sheer volume of trash removed—filling the city's largest dumpster—was cause for jubilation that cold February day in 2010. But a one-day outpouring of community support could not solve the ongoing crisis: the need for systematic, thorough maintenance.

In early May 2010, the city's Historic Preservation Commission awarded a Certificate of Appreciation to the red-vested Clampers for their decades of service repairing the cemetery's fences and clearing paths. Speaking on behalf of the group was Peter McGettigan, a Vietnam veteran and great-great-grandson of General Mariano Guadalupe Vallejo. "Some people say we are a drinking club devoted to preservation. Others say we are a preservation club devoted to drinking. Either way, we—the Branciforte chapter of E Clampus Vitus—are deeply committed to Evergreen as the embodiment of our history and the roots of who we are."

A few weeks later, the Memorial Day celebration at Evergreen drew a far larger than usual crowd. Army veteran Robert Nelson, author of *Old Soldier: The Story of the Grand Army of the Republic in Santa Cruz County*, together with the Sons of Union Veterans, was responsible for reviving the tradition. In 1999, collaborating with several veterans' organizations, they initiated the permanent return of the Memorial Day observances after a three-decade hiatus.

The conclusion of the 2010 ceremony at Evergreen focused on Nelson's newest contribution to military history, *Remembering Our Own: The Santa Cruz County Military Honor Roll*. The book, detailing 463 biographies of those who "died while on active duty in the military during times of war," represented six years of research by Nelson and several months of assistance from the MAH Publications Committee. Many relatives of those

George Pierce, in gloves and boots, participates in the "Take Back Santa Cruz" cleanup day in 2010. *Courtesy of MAH.*

The annual Memorial Day event features a military color guard leading Civil War reenactors and dozens of veterans along Evergreen Street. *Photo by Kate Clark.*

remembered, mostly newcomers to Evergreen, showed up for the GAR's program. Scores of books were sold that day, and docents fielded dozens of questions from attendees.

In stark contrast to the eloquent speeches and outpouring of support for veterans on Memorial Days, the GAR section has a distinctly forgotten feel. Uneven steps lead to tilting tombstones in disrepair. The unsightly condition had not been lost on Chuck Woodson, a member of Army Special Forces Airborne in Vietnam and longtime director of the KIA Honor Flag Organization. On first seeing the area's plight several years before, Woodson, a resident of Aptos, made his feelings known: "This is disrespectful to veterans." When he connected with Bernadette Guimarin—first sergeant, USAF Security Forces, Operation Iraqi Freedom and Operation Enduring

Freedom—they agreed to undertake a historically accurate restoration with long-term sustainability. Woodson said, "We are committed to paying our respects not only to those in the GAR section but also to the scores of veterans buried throughout Evergreen."

Executive director Figueroa, who'd gone the extra mile each year to support the Memorial Day celebrations and the veterans involved, resigned in September 2010. Looking to our future, we were unanimous as a board that the number-one priority for MAH's new leader would be to ensure financial stability. I suggested a second priority: enabling Evergreen to realize its potential as a safe and engaging outdoor classroom. Some influential trustees, art connoisseurs, disagreed. But any potential impasse over the executive director's job description unexpectedly dissolved. At a subsequent board meeting, an uninvited guest—a docent in the museum's history gallery for twenty years and former teacher—insisted we all listen up. During her long service at MAH, Judy Jones had earned considerable respect from the staff and other docents. Citing the steady stream of cutbacks to educational programs, she questioned our lack of adherence to the MAH mission: "If you aren't committed to educating, then what is the museum for?" When it came to Evergreen, Jones pulled no punches: "You own the cemetery. As the board of trustees, it is your responsibility to this entire community whether you want it or not."

It was this docent's candor and credibility that prompted the board's consensus about our number-two priority. The new executive director would support the cemetery as a consistently welcoming and positive experience. While touring Evergreen with one of the executive director candidates, Nina Simon, I felt energized listening to her assessment and upbeat conclusion: "I can't wait for my husband, Sibley [Simon], to see this." A tech entrepreneur, Sibley grew up with parents deeply committed to historic preservation. During our first conversation, he shared a telling memory of family road trips: "Storm or shine, no historical marker ever went unread!"

Before Nina took office in May 2011, Gary Neier escorted her and Sibley around the Evergreen property line with the warning, "There will be bushwhacking and poison oak." Sibley immediately replied, "I love bushwhacking." With a keen interest in local history, he began attending Evergreen Committee meetings, formally joining in July. Concurrently, Gary uploaded the Evergreen roster to FindAGrave.com and also to Ancestry.com. By dramatically increasing the number of interactions with researchers and family members, key aspects of Evergreen work became more participatory and efficient.

Meanwhile, I accepted a new role at the museum as chair of the Publications Committee, confident Evergreen was in good hands. The newly appointed trustee, Judy Jones, replaced me as the board's Evergreen liaison. She and Sibley agreed to focus on the Preservation Plan as the guide for Evergreen moving forward. At trustee meetings, Judy's lively cemetery updates earned her the nickname "Queen of Evergreen."

The committee needed a new chairperson, and in the beginning of 2012, Sibley stepped up, ready for the major challenge: a thorough clean-out, followed by relentless maintenance. City Councilwoman Cynthia Mathews—a decades-long advocate—connected him with relevant city personnel and programs. He credits then-mayor Don Lane for linking him up with participants at the Homeless Services Center (HSC, now Housing Matters). Led by HSC employee Stefan Nelson, each week six to twelve men and women experiencing homelessness joined Gary and Sibley for the first complete removal of growth in decades. Beginning at the property line adjacent to Harvey West Park, the team thoroughly scoured one section at a time. Gary described the yearlong effort: "To make regular maintenance even possible we had to remove decades of compacted debris, layer upon layer, in addition to the jungle of overgrowth."

MEETING PEOPLE WHERE THEY ARE

While the Preservation Plan spelled out dozens of goals, *how* those would be accomplished was equally important. The overall MAH methodology, including Evergreen, ensured an inclusive and fluid structure: match volunteers with *their* interests. "A certain percentage of people get so invested they work to move Evergreen forward," Sibley explains. "But first they must enjoy the experience." How could this be achieved?

Evergreen Committee members describe Sibley's style as "pragmatic prioritizing." What can we accomplish with the resources we have *now*? For example, in 2013, the hillside behind the DeLamater plot appeared on the verge of collapse—a result of campers, vandals and others determined to perch or sleep atop the adjacent Heath vault. Threatening the safety of visitors, the instability also imperiled nearby grave sites. Sibley queried the group: "Do we have the resources to tackle this?" Having recently constructed a similar wall, Gary volunteered to lead the effort. Nancy Campeau—DeLamater's great-granddaughter and a committee member

Gary Neier and Paul Steffan—a director of Housing Matters (formerly HSC)—are part of the team effort to construct a retaining wall. Sibley Simon works at the far end of the wall. *Photo by Sangye Hawke.*

since 2008—offered $1,400 for high-quality blocks, and the HSC provided essential manpower.

Within four months, a thirty-foot-long retaining wall became an attractive addition to the historic garden ambience. The concrete blocks used to create it and other permanent walls mimic the limestone blocks visible in the oldest plots. More practically, the walls hold back the steep hillsides and the ever-encroaching carpet of ivy and blackberry vines. Retaining walls from the twentieth century, mostly rotted wood from contact with the moist soil, are continually being replaced with more lasting structures.

Lighthearted camaraderie permeates the volunteers through the weekly work events, culminating in a communal lunch. It's a firmly established tradition that every week a committee member or the neighboring business Plantronics (now known as Poly) treats the crew. "Always having a hearty lunch delivered makes us feel appreciated, and it's a good time for bonding," says volunteer Frank Hayden. Melissa May, a student at Cal State University–Monterey Bay, believes it's a vital part of her service-learning internship at Evergreen: "The fellowship at lunch continues the mentoring I get during the morning of intense work."

Renewed Ambition and the Chinese Gate

In 2013, Nina Simon launched MAH's "Renewed Ambition" effort. During her presentations promoting the museum's inclusive vision, she consistently mentioned the work at Evergreen. With a large banner of the same name, Sibley brought the campaign to the cemetery grounds. He enlisted author and historian Geoffrey Dunn to share Evergreen's history with several dozen Evergreen supporters. Midway through his talk, highlighting the significance of Chinese burials, Geoffrey pointed uphill to that area: "We need to do something there." Soon after, he met with local businessman and philanthropist George Ow Jr., and an extraordinary undertaking began.

Ow's knowledge of the cemetery came from visits there with his close friend Sandy Lydon. When George revisited Evergreen in 2013, it felt like a miracle. "It was all shined up." Prior to Sibley's involvement, the cemetery and surrounding acreage had been densely overgrown. Moved by the dramatic change, Ow recalls, "As I stood there looking out from the Chinese burial ground, I envisioned something everyone could see from the road. The spirits say do not forget us, and I knew there had to be a gate in this gorgeous place." According to Lydon, the metaphorical significance of the gate is profound. Ow elaborates, "It means the opening of infinite possibilities, and that's what those buried at Evergreen did for us."

Interred at Evergreen in March 1949, George's honorary uncle, Chin Lai, spent sixty of his eighty-three years in Santa Cruz, working as a vegetable gardener and a cook in lumber mills. Along with other elderly members of the Chee Kong Tong, he lived in the old Joss House, maintaining the ever-burning light in front of the altar. Ow, who spent precious moments of his childhood in Chinatown with Chin Lai, shared these memories:

Chin Lai and his peers, the Chinese Pioneers, were sent out into the world because things in China were so bad. They were sent out to make money to send back to their families. They knew early on how tough it would be to just survive, but they did their duty. While millions of others starved to death, the money they sent home kept their families alive. Chin Lai and his fellows put up with hard times and saw most of their friends grow old and die off without ever earning enough money to return home. Only their bones would return home. And if they were one of the last ones, there would be no one to clean their bones and ship them back to their home village. Their bones would lay unclaimed. These forlorn spirits walk Evergreen and all over Santa Cruz and I feel them, the hungry ghosts.

Chin Lai told my father, "You were born at the right time." How lucky my dad was to go into the army, be respected, become a citizen, vote, own land, have a family and really become an American. He felt so lucky to live in America and be an American, at whatever level was available to him at the time. In 1982, my father told Sandy Lydon, "You must remember that compared with life in China, America was the land of opportunity, the Golden Mountain. America is still the land of opportunity." Now imagine me knowing the history and being born in 1943, the year that the Chinese Exclusion Law was stricken down, erased. I was the luckiest guy in the world. The shackles that Chin Lai and his peers and my father and his peers had would be thrown aside for me—and the others in my family younger than me. I cannot, will not ever forget this. The Chinese Gate at Evergreen would be a small symbol of what the Chinese pioneers did for me.[138]

To make this vision a reality, Sibley relied on a team of experts: George Ow, Sandy Lydon, Geoffrey Dunn and Tom Ralston of Ralston Concrete. "Initially, I was afraid I might not get it right, but we all came together." Sibley defined his job as listening to the experts and then guiding the team's process. While the gate and memorial were being constructed by Ralston's crew, the Evergreen volunteers and Clampers rebuilt a very long staircase from Evergreen Street to the memorial gate, creating improved access. All components of the area were now complete, as the city had previously installed a large and artistic drainage ditch down the hillside.

In early 2014, the "Evergreenies," as they were often called, began detailed plans for the public dedication of the Chinese Gate to be held in

Chin Lai and several other aged members of the Chee Kong Tong lived out their lives in the Freemasons' headquarters (Joss House) overlooking the San Lorenzo River. *Special Collections, University Library, UCSC, Santa Cruz County Historic Photograph Collection.*

George Ow Jr. was born in 1943, the year the Chinese Exclusion Act was finally repealed. As George looks out from the majestic Chinese Gate, Chin Lai's grave marker and several others appear in the background. *Photo by Gary Neier.*

April. The profound and moving event, called Feeding the Hungry Ghosts, created a universal feeling of caring for our ancestors and for one another. The occasion, known as *Qingming*—tomb-sweeping day—is celebrated every April by the Han Chinese. At Evergreen, the festival drew hundreds of participants and exceeded all expectations. The momentum seemed unstoppable.

WHEN THE CHIPS ARE DOWN

It was late 2013 when the *Sentinel* reported, "Evergreen Cemetery near Harvey West Park is often a hangout for the homeless, which means it's not unusual to stumble across beer bottles, cigarette butts, personal belongings, drug paraphernalia and human feces when visiting the sacred ground." In response, Nina Simon emphasized the importance of more public events at the cemetery "so that it's a welcoming place for the community rather than one overrun by transients."[139]

But the summer after the Chinese Gate dedication, negative use was on the uptick yet again. As the problem proliferated, the Evergreen Committee spent a distressing amount of time cleaning out illegal campsites, weekly filling a truck to the brim with trash. Mary Wood, having recently returned to Santa Cruz, described it as the "undoing of everything we were trying to accomplish." Sibley Simon, knowing they could only solve the problem with dedicated partners, coordinated with city park rangers, the police department, Councilwoman Mathews and MAH staff. When Dave Newcomb showed up—"outraged" that the Newcomb family plot had become a favorite place for persistent loitering and horrific debris—he learned a plan was in place. The strategic involvement of law enforcement coupled with the committee's ownership of the process closed Evergreen for renovations in August 2015. Newcomb not only joined the team but also donated needed equipment.

With their wooden barriers and signs in place at the entrances, volunteers signed up for patrols throughout the day and once every night. Kate Clark, who daily walked the area both before and after work, called the police more than once on trespassers. Very quickly, negative use tapered off and the transient population moved elsewhere. The respect and care with which the committee and city staff handled the five-month closure showed: campers had the opportunity to pick up removed belongings at a central location, and not a single injury or serious incident occurred. "We didn't solve anything related to the homeless population," according to Clark, "but we did protect Evergreen from being overrun."

Could it be sustained? Nancy Campeau was deeply concerned that the problem might resurface once the barriers came down. Fortunately, it didn't. Gary Neier, the most consistent presence at Evergreen, summarized the effect: "The closure was a last-ditch effort, and it allowed us to reset expectations."

RESTORATION

A feature in the *San Francisco Chronicle*, "Buried and Forgotten,"[140] reporting on California graveyards in need of repair, summed up major challenges facing Evergreen's stewards: "Nobody knows how many bodies were put into mass graves or interred under long-missing tombstones. Vines and poison

Piper the Forensic Dog takes a rest in front of an Evergreen grave marker. *Photo by Sangye Hawke.*

oak cover everything." The Evergreen representative in 1999 responded, referring to the Chinese section and Potters' Field: "We would love to know who's buried there. We're trying, but there's only so much volunteers can do," she said. "It's just awful."

Confronting the problem of lost graves, volunteer Sangye Hawke brought her understanding of state-of-the-art discovery procedures. Membership in the Association for Gravestone Studies provided guidance on how to use resource networks, restoration archaeologists and canine forensic teams. To help identify burial patterns, a significant factor in locating missing or misplaced graves, she visited other historic cemeteries. By 2014, Hawke's efforts were coming to fruition: confirming existing sites, identifying areas without burials and finding previously unknown ones. These discoveries helped not only the restoration of the cemetery but also the accuracy of the roster. Imagine the elation of those within earshot when Hawke, small shovel in hand and smiling, found a long-missing headstone or artifact and let out a shout!

Chapter 13

FAMILIES THEN AND NOW

O f the many accomplishments of the Evergreen Committee, the volunteers generally agree on what's been most significant: the deep clean-out of decades of compacted debris and removal of truckloads of invasive growth. Judy Jones described the visual effect: "From the GAR section you can now see the entire cemetery, and we must keep it that way." Dependable maintenance opened the way for restoring dozens of headstones and replacing lost markers. Mary Jo May, a school tour docent for fifteen years, says this major achievement has made Evergreen a "truly joyful place." Descendants who've reconnected with the cemetery or who may be connecting for the first time radiate that joy.

Clark, who works full time at a publishing company, donates about five hundred hours a year primarily compiling accurate data on families and communicating with them. To date, she's connected with over two hundred descendants; some who've received a phone call have been moved to tears. With a renewed interest in Evergreen burials, Clark focuses on how best to meet the specific needs of each family: Do they want a ceremony? Will they elect to do the digging? What would they like from the committee? The entire process can take months, and the most challenging component is the research. How accurate are the dates, the designated location, family history and spellings? Some plot-holding families, for example, may have had their names spelled three or four different ways in early media coverage and in history books.

Return to Evergreen

Theophilus Gottlieb Schupbach, an immigrant from Switzerland, Civil War veteran and former worker at Kron's Tannery, took his own life in March 1897. In a letter to the coroner, he made a final request: "I wish to be buried at Evergreen Cemetery near my sister's grave."[141] A decade later, Theo's wife, Emma Augusta Geyer Schupbach, joined him, along with their son Willie, who had passed on at age two, and Theo's sister, Marianna Schupbach Geyer.

For well over a century, the family plot was not used again. Then, in July 2018, the ashes of Vernon Schupbach, Emma and Theophilus's grandson, were reinterred at Evergreen. After a hiatus of more than a century, what had prompted the family's return?

Vernon had originally been interred in 2014 in Spokane, Washington. When his wife, Jeanette Baker Schupbach, passed on in 2017, several family members were opposed to having the couple's ashes buried in a place too distant for most to visit and without any family history. While exploring their options, relatives resonated with Evergreen's historical significance, cared-for grounds and warm reception from Kate Clark. Without question, they would move the couple's remains there. Schupbach descendants came from all over the country—New York, Louisiana, Arizona, Oregon and many parts of California—for the event.

During the ceremony, which I had the privilege of observing, I felt moved by the sincerity with which the extended family cherished their heritage. Vernon and Jeanette's son Gary, the last member of the clan to be born in Santa Cruz (at Sisters' Hospital in 1949), gave the eulogy. His tribute focused on his parents' kindness to people in need, respect for others as equals regardless of social status and emphasis on the importance of living like ladies and gentlemen. The well-beloved couple, both born and raised in Santa Cruz, had fifteen grandchildren, all of whom attended the ceremony. I invited one of them, Melissa Busby, to describe her experience:

> *The morning of the memorial, a few of us met at Evergreen to discuss details of the ceremony. It was my first time seeing the graves of Theophilus and Emma, my great-great-grandparents. Having learned so much about their lives through genealogy research, I was excited to "meet" them. Some of us helped the Evergreen Committee, taking turns hand-digging the hole in which my grandparents would be buried, which also added to this special event. While I am not religious and the faiths of my family members vary, we were all moved by my uncle Gary's eulogy.*

Right: Emma Geyer Schupbach passed on at age forty-four, joining her husband and son in the family plot. The next family burial took place more than a century later. *Schupbach family collection.*

Below: Hailing from all over the country, thirty members of the extended Schupbach family gather at Evergreen for the reinterment ceremony at their family plot. *Schupbach family collection.*

It truly felt like my grandparents had been united with my great-great-grandparents. The feeling of unity I experienced that day, for both the living and the deceased, has stayed with me. I often think about the history and beauty of my family and of Evergreen Cemetery, the complex life stories of the family members interred there, and the continuation of those stories through all of us and through future generations.[142]

Gary and Melissa report that several family members have expressed interest in someday being buried in the Schupbach plot at Evergreen.

TRIBUTE TO A NATIVE SON

No one knows for sure when or how headstones and markers went missing. Was their disappearance from natural causes, vandalism or some combination? Several markers have been replaced, and in August 2019, Clark, assisted by another volunteer, Frank Hayden, managed the installation of a new metal marker. The replacement of Matías Lorenzana's 1915 marker celebrates the extraordinary origin and longevity of one of our county's earliest families.

Today, the Lorenzana family has resided in Santa Cruz County for almost two hundred years. Available records, though scant, trace their origin to Mexico City in 1800. Turning back the clock to that place and time, imagine being a ten-year-old boy living in the Royal House for Abandoned Children. You are officially identified as *Mestizo* on the census, though you believe yourself to be of pure Aztec descent. Your surname, Lorenzana, is shared by all the orphans living at the Royal House to honor the former archbishop of Mexico, Francisco Antonio de Lorenzana y Burton. When he (the prelate) decides that you, Macedonio, and nineteen other "Lorenzana" children will be sent to Alta California in 1810, he has a very specific purpose: to help expand the population of Mexican settlers.

Once in California, Macedonio had the good fortune to be raised by Francisco Castro of the well-established San Jose family and to marry María Romulda Vásquez, daughter of a soldier and a neophyte. The couple first lived at the San Francisco Presido, and then—after his service in the Mexican army—they settled in Santa Cruz. One of nine Californio families owning land in Branciforte, they were described as "steady" and part of "the close-knit community, eventually growing to include at least a dozen children."[143] María and Macedonio's son Matías arrived in 1828 and received holy baptism at the mission.

Macedonio, a public official during the administration of Governor José Figueroa, was promoted to the rank of second alcalde in 1841, sharing the responsibility for land grants and general government business. After losing that position during the Mexican-American War, however, his status in the community dwindled. American law denied the benefits of citizenship to persons of "Indian" blood. Consequently, Macedonio was not permitted to testify in boundary disputes about deeds that he had authorized.

The now-grown Matías and his wife, Concepción Rodríguez, farmed their land, first in Branciforte and by 1870 in the more remote neighborhood of Happy Valley. Although several of their relatives had become outlaws, the couple and their children lived a relatively quiet life. But that all changed on the night of September 10, 1871. Tiburcio Vásquez, one of the most notorious and colorful banditos, wanted for stagecoach robbery, appeared in Santa Cruz County. After shooting out several windows in a Branciforte bordello, he and his men engaged in a gunfight in downtown Santa Cruz, injuring a lawman. Fleeing town, Vásquez—with a wound in his chest—knew he could count on his second cousin Matías to shelter him and his desperado companions. When they arrived at the Lorenzana farm, Concepción dressed the wound and Matías hid the fugitives in a nearby ravine and in his barn.

The posse arrived on the evening of September 13. After an extensive search, they discovered the outlaws when Matías's six-year-old son, Jesús, inadvertently disclosed their whereabouts in the barn. A shootout ensued, and Deputy Sheriff Roberto Majors, from the prominent Castro family, killed Vásquez's companion, Francisco Barcenas. Vásquez, hiding outside, managed to escape. Matías had no such luck; Undersheriff Charlie Lincoln, known as the "boy sheriff," jailed Matías that very night.

Matías was incarcerated in this supposedly secure jail on the upper plaza. With the razing of the building in 1906, John Bilodeau repurposed the granite-block walls for tombstones. *Courtesy of MAH.*

Matías feared that he might be killed before being brought to trial, a fate that had befallen his nephew Pedro Lorenzana, who had been taken from the jail six years before and never seen again. In the early morning of September 21, ten masked men broke into the county jail, bound and gagged the guard and rode away with Matías. Some speculated that the intruders were members of Matt Tarpey's Watsonville gang; others suspected Santa Cruzans, including Charlie Lincoln. The vigilantes returned Matías to the scene of the crime and hanged him from a tree in the middle of his farm. But as fate would have it, the dying man's friend and neighbor Dave Boffman— an ex-slave—arrived and cut him down.[144]

From then on, Matías and his relatives were wary—on the lookout for vigilantes. When a teenage member of the extended Vásquez family was locked up in 1885, Matías, gun in hand, stood guard with the boy's family outside the jail. He continued to live in the Blackburn Gulch area and, consistent with the changing economy, left farming to become a lumberman. But his son Jesús Lorenzana and grandson George embraced the vaquero way of life, working at the Cowell Ranch (now part of the UC–Santa Cruz campus), where George became the foreman.

Pictured at the Cowell Ranch are Jesús and George Lorenzana, son and grandson of Matías. "Fabulous horsemen" is how historian Phil Reader described them. *Courtesy of Jim Lorenzana.*

Left: Jim Lorenzana delights in the new marker for his great-grandfather Matías Lorenzana, installed in 2019. No one knows when the original went missing. *Photo by Susan Krevitt.*

Below: Born in Branciforte in 1828, Matías Lorenzana was interred at Evergreen in 1915. Three subsequent generations of Lorenzanas have made Santa Cruz their home. *Photo by Gary Neier.*

Matías led a full life that extended well into his eighties. Six pallbearers participated in his 1915 funeral, and members of the Congregational church choir offered hymns.[145] But why did he select Evergreen instead of the Catholic cemetery, where almost all his siblings were buried? While that mystery remains, the recognition of Matías's final resting place brings a deep sense of completion and connection for his great-grandson Jim Lorenzana. A lifelong resident of Live Oak, Jim, who had a thirty-year career with Santa Cruz County, recalls that when he was ten years old, his father, George, took him "to the Evergreen area where blacks and Chinese were buried." Together they tried to locate the Lorenzana grave site, but a marker no longer existed. Today, its replacement does.

Determining the right placement for the Lorenzana marker became a challenge. Ultimately, Clark had to decide that an approximate location, based on all available information, was good enough. With the approval of both MAH and the family, she experienced firsthand what it meant to Jim Lorenzana to have such a vital part of his history recognized. "To pay respect to persons long gone, who may or may not have anyone to remember them today is a remarkably and endearingly satisfying honor," says Clark. "I feel proud to help bring their stories back to light; it says you were here, you made a difference, you were part of Santa Cruz."

A PERPETUAL ARCH

A century ago, the Potrero land, later the Imus orchard, had yet to become an industrial area. At that time, Worthy and DeEtte Newcomb, committed to celebrating the beauty of the burial ground, donated an arch in memory of the two children they had lost decades earlier in Nebraska. In the fall of 2019, their three great-grandchildren restored the original structure.

Dave Newcomb describes how the new arch came to be:

To tell you the truth, all my life I have known about our family connection to Evergreen Cemetery, but in my youth I did not have much interest. During the last several years when I have seen how so many people, for so many years, have been so dedicated to the restoration and upkeep, I not only began to appreciate their efforts but also Evergreen itself. When I heard through the Evergreen Committee updates that the arch was in danger of falling— due to massive amounts of rust—I knew it was time for the Newcomb

Some portions of the old Imus farm and orchard continued to be cultivated. The white posts of the Evergreen arch, installed by the Newcombs in the early 1920s, are at center rear. *Special Collections, University Library, UCSC, Santa Cruz County Historic Photograph Collection.*

Left to right: Ashley Holding, DeEtte Johnson, Leslie Newcomb and Karen Ammon paint the rebuilt Newcomb arch, installed in October 2019. *Photo by Gary Neier.*

On a regular weekly workday, a group of Evergreen volunteers gather before lunch. *Left to right*: Wendell Read, Anne Hayden, Sibley Simon, Bob Dahlgren, Cynthia Mathews, Nancy Campeau, Frank Hayden, Ken Gilbert, Kate Clark, Gary Neier, Melissa May and Tom Cannell. Sitting in the front row are Farley and Posey. *Photo by Traci Bliss.*

family to step up. My sister Leslie and my cousin DeEtte, named for our great-grandmother, joined me as active participants in the arch restoration. I can say that it feels right and good, and that I feel a connection to my family, dead and alive, that I had not known before.[146]

Karen Ammon, Dave's niece and DeEtte's great-great-granddaughter, watched with me when the original arch came down in mid-2019. She told me about her decision some years ago to be married at close-by Harvey West Park. While describing what that proximity meant to her, it sounded like she was speaking for so many Evergreen families—those who've returned as well as those who never left. "We all share a profound sense of continuity."

EPILOGUE

The way we treat our cemetery is a reflection of our contemporary community;
it is a mirror on our values.
—Sandy Lydon

D uring Evergreen's first fifty years, burials memorialized many of the families who had transformed Santa Cruz from a village into a bustling town. The vibrant Victorian garden, often referred to then as the pioneer cemetery, easily kept pace with the community's progress. By contrast, the twentieth century ushered in a discouragingly repetitive cycle. Each successive rescue mission tried to counter the steady decline in interments and concurrent loss of interest. Was the struggle for Evergreen's survival a futile endeavor? A decade ago, I was tempted to say yes, recalling the Greek myth of King Sisyphus, who was assigned to perpetually roll a rock up a hill only to have it tumble back down each time he approached the top.

Undeniably, each new effort to restore the cemetery appeared to lose ground when the basic upkeep could not be sustained. But as I delved deeply into the history, a comparison to Sisyphus eroded. Amid an invasive and stifling overgrowth of briers, brambles and poison oak, one hundred years of advocacy achieved quiet victories for Evergreen: incorporating as a legal entity in the 1920s; acquiring the extension in the 1940s; receiving state designation as a place of historical interest in the 1960s; joining the Santa Cruz County Historical Trust in the 1980s; and producing a Preservation

Plan in 2010. Each of these accomplishments contributed to the radical renovation of the last decade, including the future installation of sidewalk-quality paths and more accessible parking.

As the Sisyphus analogy dissolved, a new one has emerged as I've watched Evergreen flourish. Whether during weekly workdays or at special events, I feel an energetic artistry at each visit. It recalls the painstaking work of medieval artists whose efforts set the stage for the Italian Renaissance—an era of bold breakthroughs and continued creativity. So, too, with Evergreen's Renaissance.

What a privilege to join with the spirit of my Imus ancestors—cattle ranchers and fruit farmers who donated their land—and cheer a century of volunteers who have cherished this burial ground as much as its originators.

Evergreen is a treasured historical landmark of Santa Cruz County, and this publication honors and ensures its preservation as a special place in our local history.

—Robb Woulfe
Executive Director, Museum of Art and History, 2020

Appendix I

PLOT ROSTER

This list can be used with a map of Evergreen plot numbers to find locations of those families and individuals included in the text.

Amner, Edgar	229
Amner, Thomas	229
Anthony, Asa	115
Arcan, John and Abigail (Miller) and children Julia and Charles	214
Archer, Mary	24
Asisara, Lorenzo	Old Section
Bachelder, Charles and LaSalle (Banker) and children Celeste and John Arthur	239
Bilodeau, John and Laura (Blanchard)	74
Blackburn, William and Harriet (Mead) and son Fredrick	66
Blanchard, Seth and Albetina (Labish) and children Seth Jr., Albert, Albertina Westfall	179
Boston, Joseph and Eliza (Bull) and son William	153
Case, Benjamin, Mary Amney (White) and Rollin	1

Chester, George Andrew	Old Section
Chin Lai	Chinese Section
Cooper, William	113
DeLamater, GBV and Eliza (Cope) and daughter Maria	170–71
Dormer, Belle (Smith)	191
Dunlap, Orie and Edna (Bilodeau) and brother Clyde	180
Errington, Joseph	24
Errington, Landreth	24
Flores, Abby (Arcan)	214
Geyer, Marianna (Schupbach)	124
Gharkey, David	152
Graham, Isaac	83
Harrell, Chauncey	191
Heath, Frank and Lillian (Dake) and parents Lucian and Jane (Edwards)	172
Hecox, James Monroe	56
Hicks, Achilles and son Jesse	56
Hicks, Grace (Archer), formerly Grace Errington	24
Hunter, Katherine (Imus)	80
Imus, Charles	62
Imus, Hiram Jr. and Eliza (Collins)	80
Imus, Hiram Sr. and Ruth (Palmer)	62
Imus, James	80
Jordan, Albion and Mary (Perry) Fagen, formerly Mary Jordan	142
Kilfoyl, Clifford and Edith (Williamson)	170
Kittredge, Francis and Almira (Mead) and children Ruel and Marietta	155
Labish, Johan Carl and Augusta (Kattengel)	178

Lem Sam	Chinese Section
Lorenzana, Matías	Old Section
Lou Sing	Chinese Section
Nelson, London (aka Loudon)	6
Newcomb, Worthy and DeEtte (Alderman)	148
Perry, Charles and Della (Pierce) and father John B.	141
Pilkington, Thomas and Mary Caroline	41
Prewitt, James	145
Rawson, Asa	176
Rice, Henry and Lucy (Imus)	102
Schupbach, Theophilus and Emma (Geyer) and son Willie	124
Schupbach, Vernon and Jeanette (Baker)	124
Speel, Henry	67
Storey, Judge William and Eliza (Dufour)	206
Taylor, Arthur and Mary (Prescott)	158
Taylor, Nelson	158
Tefertiller, Earl and Ruby (Dunlap)	180
Thompson, Uriah and Charlotte (Rice) and children Frances Minerva and Henry	89
Wilkerson, Grayson	132
Williams, James and Mary (Patterson) and sons James A. and Andrew J.	161
Williamson, William and Grace (Delamater)	158
Wong Kee and Mrs. Wong Kee	Chinese Section

THE SOCIETY OF CALIFORNIA PIONEERS OF SANTA CRUZ COUNTY

This list can be used with a map of Evergreen plot numbers to find locations of those members buried at Evergreen. The *Santa Cruz County History Journal #4* contains biographical information for each individual.

Charles Arcan (1848–1907), arrived in CA 1848	214
Seth Blanchard (1822–1889), arrived in CA 1849	179
Eliza Bull Boston (1832–1820), arrived in CA 1861	153
Rollin Dwight Case (1844–1908), arrived in CA 1847	1
Henry Doane (1811–1894), arrived in CA 1849	Plot unknown
John Dreher (1814–1885), arrived in CA 1847	123
Joseph Gallapher (1814–1893), arrived in CA 1849	Plot unknown
Charles Hodgdon (1814–1894), arrived in CA 1849	Plot unknown
Stephen Howard Hunt (1826–1890), arrived in CA 1849	212
Katherine Collins Imus Hunter (1840–1927), arrived in CA 1850	80
Alfred Russell Imus (1844–1895), arrived in CA 1849	102

Edmund Jones (1827–1903), arrived in CA 1849	156
William McElroy (1816–1897), arrived in CA 1849	224
Daniel Monteath (1820 or 1821–1882), arrived in CA 1837	Masonic section
Chester Winans Peck (1820–1910), arrived in CA 1849	Plot unknown
Charles Casper Perry (1845–1933), arrived in CA 1853	141
James Levy Prewitt (1826–1893), arrived in CA 1849	145
Reuben Haywood Sawin (1802–1884), arrived in CA 1849	159
William Henry Seaver (1823–1895), arrived in CA 1849	Plot unknown
Herbert Nelson Taylor (1859–1927), arrived in CA n/a	158
Nelson Taylor (1811–1898), arrived in CA 1850	158
Charlotte Rice Thompson (1835–1916), arrived in CA 1852	89
Uriah Williams Thompson (1830–1903), arrived in CA 1849	89
Henry Whinery (1830–1920), arrived in CA 1850	5
Joseph Nelson Williamson (1818–1897), arrived in CA 1850	Plot unknown

NOTES

Chapter 1

1. Elliott, *Santa Cruz County*, 6.
2. Harrison, *History of Santa Cruz County*, 21.

Chapter 2

3. Robinson, *Life in California*, 21.
4. Graham deposition, May 1840.
5. *The Southron*, January 5, 1843.
6. Stewart, *California Trail*, 45–46.
7. *San Jose Pioneer*, July 1881.
8. Stewart, *California Trail*, 71.
9. *San Jose Pioneer*, July 1881
10. *Forgotten Journey*.
11. Clyman, *American Frontiersman*.
12. Larkin to Bolcoff, November 19, 1845.
13. Bolcoff to Larkin, December 4, 1845.
14. *Santa Cruz Sentinel*, August 5, 1869.
15. Pokriots, *California Bound*.
16. *Riptide*, November 1950, 6.
17. *Alta California*, August 30, 1860.

18. *Pittsburgh Gazette*, June 10, 1845.
19. Aram, "Across the American Continent," 623.
20. Ibid., 627.
21. Ibid.
22. *Joliet Signal*, November 17, 1846.
23. *Alcalde Deed*, March 3, 1850.

Chapter 3

24. Hempton, *Methodism*, 153.
25. *Santa Cruz County History Journal* 4, 35.
26. Manly, *Death Valley in '49*, 3.
27. Jensen, *1849 Death Valley Pioneers*, 20.
28. Latta, *Death Valley 49ers*, 24.
29. Jensen, *1849 Death Valley Pioneers*, 23.
30. Hunter in *Riptide*, December 21, 1950, 5–6.
31. *LA Times*, September 6, 1908.
32. Ibid.
33. *Sacramento Union*, September 16, 1853.
34. *Pacific Sentinel*, August 30, 1856.
35. *Santa Cruz Sentinel*, June 15, 1898.
36. Harrison, *History of Santa Cruz County*, 22–23.
37. Farnham, *California, Indoors and Out*, 469.
38. Ibid., 471.
39. *Santa Cruz Sentinel*, October 6, 1885.

Chapter 4

40. Rowland, *Santa Cruz: The Early Years*, 206.
41. *San Jose Tribune*, May 12, 1856.
42. *Pacific Sentinel*, June 20, 1857.
43. Ibid., June 4, 1858.
44. Ibid., June 11, 1858.
45. Santa Cruz County Deeds, June 7, 1858.
46. *Santa Cruz Sentinel*, March 21, 1863.
47. Koch, *Santa Cruz County: Parade of the Past*, 21.

Chapter 5

48. 1850 Census.
49. *New Orleans Picayune*, March 7, 1852.
50. *Alta California*, September 23, 1853.
51. *Sacramento Union*, October 21, 1853.
52. Ibid., May 24, 1854.
53. *Pacific Sentinel*, August 1, 1857.
54. Reader, *Brief Biography of London Nelson*.
55. *Pacific Sentinel*, May 18, 1860.
56. *Santa Cruz History Journal* 4, 235–36.
57. *Santa Cruz Sentinel*, May 19, 1903.
58. Ibid., February 5, 1916.
59. Chace, *Sidewalk Companion*, 56.
60. Grace Errington Memoir.
61. *Santa Cruz Sentinel*, May 13, 1865.
62. Ibid., June 24, 1865.
63. Ibid., March 18, 1876.
64. Ibid., May 20, 1955.
65. Ibid., June 18, 1881.
66. Ibid., May 20, 1955.
67. Ibid., October 28, 1920.
68. Lydon, *Chinese Gold*, 281.

Chapter 6

69. *Santa Cruz Sentinel*, September 5, 1861.
70. Ibid., October 10, 1861.
71. Ibid., November 1861.
72. Ibid., August 15, 1863.
73. Ibid., May 22, 1869.
74. *Santa Cruz Courier Item*, June 2, 1880.
75. Ibid., June 1, 1882.
76. *Santa Cruz Sentinel*, May 10, 1885.

Chapter 7

77. Adam, "Rare Old Books in the Bishop's Library."
78. *Santa Cruz Surf*, September 26, 1891.
79. Harrison, *History of Santa Cruz County*, 47.
80. *Santa Cruz Sentinel*, February 25, 1908 (Sexton), and October 8, 1932 (E.L. Williams).
81. Ibid., March 26, 1881.
82. Ibid., May 14, 1881.
83. Ibid., November 11, 1888.
84. Ibid., July 29, 1890.
85. Ibid., June 23, 1892.
86. Ibid., August 29, 1900.
87. For a detailed account of Henry and Lottie Dame Thompson, see Hyman, "History of Carmelita Cottages."
88. For a detailed account of the Boston family, see Bagshaw, *Santa Cruz History Journal* 8.
89. *Santa Cruz Evening News*, March 12, 1908.

Chapter 8

90. Reprinted in *Santa Cruz Sentinel*, May 24, 1936.
91. *Santa Cruz Sentinel*, February 13, 1936.
92. *San Francisco Chronicle*, August 16, 1896.
93. *Santa Cruz Sentinel*, December 21, 1937.
94. Koch, *Santa Cruz County: Parade of the Past*, 290.
95. Gudnason, *Rings in the Redwoods*, 103.
96. *Santa Cruz Sentinel*, January 12, 1900.
97. *Santa Cruz History Journal* 4, 51.
98. *Santa Cruz Evening News*, April 13, 1917.
99. Ibid., August 12, 1925.
100. Campeau, *Journal of G.B.V. DeLamater*.
101. *Santa Cruz Surf*, December 21, 1896.
102. *Santa Cruz Evening News*, July 16, 1915.

Chapter 9

103. *Santa Cruz Surf*, September 9, 1884.
104. *Santa Cruz Sentinel*, September 13, 1884.
105. Lydon, *Chinese Gold*, 271.
106. *Santa Cruz Sentinel*, January 2, 1886.
107. Lydon, *Chinese Gold*, 272.
108. *Santa Cruz Sentinel*, December 1, 1886.
109. Ibid., April 24, 1887.
110. Ibid., December 5, 1954.
111. Ibid., August 4, 1893.
112. Ibid., January 7, 1900.
113. *Santa Cruz Surf*, February 2, 1901.
114. Ibid., February 26, 1901.
115. Ibid., January 26, 1912.
116. *Santa Cruz Sentinel*, November 24, 1926.
117. Ibid.
118. Santa Cruz County burial permits.

Chapter 10

119. *Santa Cruz History Journal* 4, 51.
120. *Santa Cruz Sentinel*, September 2, 1882.
121. Notes of Ruby Tefertiller interview with Albertina Blanchard.
122. *Santa Cruz Sentinel*, February 14, 1958.

Chapter 11

123. *Santa Cruz Evening News*, August 21, 1922.
124. Ibid., August 24, 1925.
125. *Santa Cruz Sentinel*, February 7, 1965.
126. Ibid., March 10, 1957.
127. Conversation with Frank Zwart, July 2019.
128. *Santa Cruz Sentinel*, June 12, 1974.
129. Conversation with Sandy Lydon, September 2019.
130. Letter from Sandy Lydon, August 2019.

131. *Santa Cruz County Historical Trust Newsletter*, May 1988.
132. *Santa Cruz Sentinel*, May 24, 1873.
133. Phil Reader, *Sentinel*, May 26, 1993.
134. *Santa Cruz Sentinel*, June 30, 1883.
135. Ibid., September 8, 1899.
136. *Santa Cruz Evening News*, April 23, 1914.

Chapter 12

137. Evergreen Preservation Plan, 27.
138. Letter from George Ow Jr., July 2019.
139. *Santa Cruz Sentinel*, October 24, 2013.
140. *San Francisco Chronicle*, October 30, 1999.

Chapter 13

141. *Santa Cruz Sentinel*, March 27, 1899.
142. Letter from Melissa Busby, August 2019.
143. Rizzo, *Santa Cruz County History Journal* 8, 23.
144. The narrative is based on the work of Phil Reader and John Boessenecker.
145. *Santa Cruz Sentinel*, June 2, 1915.
146. Letter from Dave Newcomb, August 2019.

BIBLIOGRAPHY

Books

Bancroft, H.H. *California Pastoral 1769–1848*. San Francisco: History Company, 1888.

Birnbaum, et al. *Harvesting Our Heritage*. Santa Cruz, CA: Museum of Art and History, 2017.

Bliss, Traci, and Randall Brown. *Santa Cruz's Seabright*. Charleston, SC: Arcadia Publishing, 2017.

Boessenecker, John. *Bandido: The Life and Times of Tiburcio Vasquez*. Norman: University of Oklahoma Press, 2010.

Bosso, Robert, et al. *A Legal History of Santa Cruz*. Santa Cruz, CA: Museum of Art and History, 2006.

Bunnett, Sara, and Marion Pokriots, eds. *Record Books of the Alcaldes of Santa Cruz*. Santa Cruz, CA: Genealogical Society of Santa Cruz, 1992.

Bunnett, Sara, Rick Hyman and Tina Slosberg. *Every Structure Tells a Story*. Santa Cruz, CA: S.C. Historical Trust, 1990.

Campeau, Nancy. *Journal of G.B.V. DeLamater*. Santa Cruz, CA: self-published, 2015.

Chace, John. *The Sidewalk Companion to Santa Cruz Architecture*. Santa Cruz, CA: Paper Vision Press, 1976.

Chang, Gordon H. *Ghosts of Gold Mountain: The Epic Story of the Chinese Who Built the Transcontinental Railroad*. Boston: Houghton Mifflin, 2019.

Clark, Donald T. *Santa Cruz County Place Names*. Scotts Valley, CA: Kestrel Press, 2008.

Clyman, James. *American Frontiersman, 1792–1881: The Adventures of a Trapper and Covered Wagon Emigrant as Told in His Own Reminiscences and Diaries.* San Francisco: California Historical Society, 1928.

Davis, William J. *Illustrated History of Sacramento County, California.* Chicago: Lewis Publishing Co., 1896.

Dunn, Geoffrey. "Romance of the Landscape: Santa Cruz and the California Plein Air Movement." In *Native Son: Contemporary Landscape Paintings of the California Central Coast*, by Ed Penniman. Santa Cruz, CA: Santa Cruz County Bank Art Collaborative, 2018.

————. *Santa Cruz Is in the Heart #2.* Capitola, CA: Capitola Books, 2013.

Elliott, W.W. *Santa Cruz County, California.* San Francisco: Wallace Elliott and Co., 1879.

Englehardt, Zephryin. *The Missions and Missionaries of California.* Santa Barbara, CA: Mission Santa Barbara, 1930.

Farnham, Eliza W. *California, Indoors and Out.* New York: Dix, Edwards and Co., 1856.

Farnham, Thomas J. *Life, Travels, and Adventures in California.* New York: W.H. Graham, 1847.

Gudnason, Kay. *Rings in the Redwoods: The Story of Mt. Hermon Association.* Mount Hermon, CA: Mount Hermon Association, 1972.

Harrison, E.S. *History of Santa Cruz County California.* San Francisco: Pacific Press Publishing, 1892.

Hempton, David. *Methodism: Empire of the Spirit.* New Haven, CT: Yale Press, 2005.

Jensen, Mary, and Marvin Jensen. *The Death Valley Pioneers.* N.p.: Death Valley 49ers, 2005.

Koch, Margaret. *Santa Cruz County: Parade of the Past.* Fresno, CA: Valley Publishers, 1973.

Larkin, Thomas. *The Larkin Papers.* Vol. 3. Berkeley: University of California Press, 1951–68.

Latta, Frank. *Death Valley 49ers.* Santa Cruz, CA: Bear State, 1979.

Leonard, Zenas. *Narrative of the Adventures of Zenas Leonard.* Clearfield, PA: D.W. Moore, 1839.

Lydon, Sandy. *Chinese Gold: The Chinese in the Monterey Bay Region.* Capitola, CA: Capitola Book Co., 1985.

Manly, William Lewis. *Death Valley in '49.* San Jose, CA: Pacific Tree and Vine Co., 1894.

Mora-Torres, Gregorio. *Californio Voices: The Oral Memoirs of Jose Maria Amador and Lorenzo Asisara.* Denton: University of North Texas Press, 2005.

Nelson, Robert. *Old Soldier: The Story of the G.A.R. in Santa Cruz Co.* Santa Cruz, CA: Museum of Art and History, 2004.

————. *Remembering Our Own.* Santa Cruz, CA: Museum of Art and History, 2010.

Nunis, Doyce. *The Trials of Isaac Graham.* Los Angeles: Dawson Bookshop, 1967.

Poitevin, Norman. *Guide to Old Holy Cross Cemetery.* Santa Cruz, CA: self-published, 2016.

Pokriots, Marion D. *California Bound: The Hitchcock-Patterson Saga.* Scotts Valley, CA: self-published, 1994.

Robinson, Alfred. *Life in California during a Residence of Several Years in that Territory.* New York: Wiley and Putnam, 1846.

Rowland, Leon. *Santa Cruz: The Early Years.* Santa Cruz, CA: Paper Vision Press, 1980.

Santa Cruz First Congregational Church. *A Century of Christian Witness.* Santa Cruz, CA: Sentinel Printers, 1963.

————. *Records Index, 1952–1975.* Santa Cruz, CA: S.C. Genealogical Society, 1990.

Stewart, George R. *The California Trail: An Epic with Many Heroes.* San Francisco: McGraw Hill, 1962.

Swasey, William F. *Early Days and Men of California.* Oakland, CA: Pacific Press Publishing, 1891.

Taylor, Arthur A. *California State Redwood Park.* Sacramento, CA: State Printing, 1912.

Tefertiller, Casey. *Wyatt Earp: The Life Behind the Legend.* New York: John Wiley & Sons, 1997.

Thompson and West. *History of Nevada.* Oakland, CA: Thompson and West, 1881.

Torchiana, H.A.W. *The Story of the Mission Santa Cruz.* San Francisco: P. Elder, 1933.

Thesis/Dissertation

Rizzo, Martin. "No Somos Animales: Indigenous Survival and Perseverance in 19th Century Santa Cruz, California." PhD diss., University of California–Santa Cruz, 2016.

Magazine Articles

Adam, Joaquin. "Rare Old Books in the Bishop's Library." *Historical Society of California* 5 (n.d.): 154–56.

Aram, Joseph. "Across the American Continent in a Caravan." *Journal of American History* (1907): 617–32.

Fong, Kum Ngon. "The Chinese Six Companies." *Out West Magazine*, May 1894, 518–26.

Leeds, B. Frank. "Evergreen Cemetery: Tombstones in the Old Cemetery." *New England Historical and Genealogical Society*, 1891.

Loomis, A.W. "Chinese Funeral Baked Meat." *Overland Monthly*, July 1869, 21–29.

———. "The Chinese Six Companies." *Overland Monthly*, September 1868, 558–65.

———. "Chinese Women in California." *Overland Monthly*, April 1869, 344–51.

Masters, Frederic J. "Among the Highbinders: An Account of Chinese Secret Societies." *Californian Illustrated Magazine*, January 1892, 62–74.

Steen, Judith. "The Jordans: Family with a Limerock Foundation." *Lime Kiln Chronicles* (Fall/Winter 2009).

Valhasky, Marie. "The Story of Margaret M. Hecox." *Overland Monthly*, May 1892, 535–47.

Pamphlets

Errington/Hicks, Grace. "Memoirs." Unpublished, 1915.

Koch, Margaret, ed. *Towards Artistic Development: The Legacy of Frank and Lillian Heath.* Santa Cruz Art League, 1987.

Silva, Nikki. *Art and Artists in Santa Cruz: A Historic Survey.* Santa Cruz City Museum, 1973.

Video

Forgotten Journey: The Stephens-Townsend-Murphy Saga. Forgotten Journey Productions, Toluca Lake, CA, 2001.

Journals

Santa Cruz County History Journal 3, "Branciforte Edition." Santa Cruz: Museum of Art and History, 1997.

Santa Cruz County History Journal 4, "Society of California Pioneers." Santa Cruz: Museum of Art and History, 1998.

Santa Cruz County History Journal 7, "A Split History: Redwood Logging and Conservation." Santa Cruz: Museum of Art and History, 2014.

Santa Cruz County History Journal 8, "Do You Know My Name." Santa Cruz: Museum of Art and History, 2016.

Santa Cruz County History Journal 9, "Landscapes." Santa Cruz: Museum of Art and History, 2018.

Reports

Evergreen Preservation Committee. *Evergreen Cemetery Preservation Plan.* Santa Cruz, 2009.

Newspapers

Daily Alta California (San Francisco)
Pacific Sentinel (Monterey, Santa Cruz)
Pajaro Times (Watsonville, Santa Cruz)
Riptide (Santa Cruz)
Sacramento Union
San Francisco Call
San Francisco Chronicle
San Francisco Examiner
San Jose Pioneer
Santa Cruz Courier Item
Santa Cruz Evening News
Santa Cruz Local Item
Santa Cruz Sentinel
Santa Cruz Surf

Online Archives

California Digital Newspapers (Cdnc.ucr.edu).

Newspapers.com (various titles).

Hyman, Rick. "History of the Carmelita Cottages." Santacruzpl.org, 1996.

Reader, Phil. "A Brief Biography of London Nelson." SantaCruzmah.org.

———. "To Know My Name: A History of African Americans in Santa Cruz County." Santacruzmah.org.

Rowland, Leon. Card File (library.ucsc.edu).

Tutwiler, Paul. "Notes on the History of Williams Mill and Williams Landing." Santacruzpl.org, 2000.

Interviews by Traci Bliss, October 2018–September 2019, Santa Cruz, California

Karen Amon, Nancy Campeau, Kate Clark, Sangye Hawke, Lynn Hill, Rick Hyman, Judy Jones, Jim Lorenzana, Sandy Lydon, Cynthia Mathews, Mary Jo May, Melissa May, Rachel McKay, Gary Neier, Robert Nelson, Marla Novo, George Ow Jr., Pastor Jay Pierce, Marion Pokriots, Sibley Simon, Stan Stevens, Casey Tefertiller, Mary Wood, Chuck Woodson.

INDEX

INDEX

Thompson, Frances 50, 66
Thompson, Henry 65, 66, 67, 75,
    78
Thompson, Uriah 50
Thompson, Uriah M. 106, 109
Tomasso, Enrico de. *See*
    Thompson, Henry
Trabing, Wally 112

V

Vásquez family 144
Vásquez, Tiburcio 143

W

Westfall, Albertina Blanchard 103
Wilkerson, Grayson 105
Willett, Mahlon 94
Williams family 19, 23
Williams, James 19, 22, 23, 48
Williams, Mary Patterson 17, 20,
    22, 23
Williamson, Grace DeLamater 87,
    88, 99, 111
Williamson, William 87
Winnemucca, Sarah 41
Wong Kee 89, 90, 91, 92, 93, 95,
    96
Wong Kee, Mrs. 90
Wood, Mary 118, 121, 136
Woodson, Chuck 128
Woo Gap 95
Woulfe, Robb 150

Y

Yelland, Raymond D. 75

Z

Zayante 19, 22, 24, 41

ABOUT THE AUTHORS

Traci Bliss, an emerita professor of education, served as a policy advisor to the National Board for Professional Teaching Standards during her academic career. In that context, she received national and international awards for her documentary films of accomplished teachers. Bliss retired early to write the untold stories of women who helped shape Santa Cruz County in the late nineteenth and early twentieth centuries. She serves on the Santa Cruz Historic Preservation Commission, leads history tours at Henry Cowell Redwoods State Park and helps select Rotary scholarship recipients. Her ancestors, the Imus family, donated land for Evergreen Cemetery in 1858, and Bliss is the seventh generation of Imus women to live in Santa Cruz. Her BA, MA and PhD degrees are from Stanford, and she holds an MPA from the LBJ School, University of Texas at Austin. She is a lifetime member of the Society of California Pioneers.

Randall Brown, a Santa Cruz County Distinguished Historian, coauthored with Bliss the best-selling *Santa Cruz's Seabright*. They've also co-written several articles featured in *A Split History: Redwood Logging and Conservation in the Santa Cruz Mountains*. Brown, also an expert on the history of silent films, specializes in films made in the San Lorenzo Valley and serves as a regular history columnist for the San Lorenzo/Scotts Valley *Press Banner*. He is a graduate of Wesleyan University and holds a BA degree in American studies.

Visit us at
www.historypress.com